Homosexuality
in the
Horoscope

Karl Gunter Heimsoth, M.D.

ISBN-10: 0-86690-113-2
ISBN-13: 978-0-86690-113-0

Translator: Richard S. Baldwin
Cover Design: Jack Cipolla

Published by:
American Federation of Astrologers, Inc.
6535 S. Rural Road
Tempe, AZ 85283

www.astrologers.com

Contents

Going our own way. When we take the decisive step and make up our minds to follow our own path, a secret is suddenly revealed to us: It is clear that all those who had hitherto been friendly to us and on intimate terms with us judged themselves to be superior to us, and are offended now. The best among them are indulgent and are content to wait patiently until we once more find the "right path"—they know it, apparently. Others make fun of us and pretend that we have been seized with a temporary attack of mild insanity, or spitefully point out some seducer. The more malicious say we are vain fools and do their best to blacken our motives; while the worst of all see in us their greatest enemy—someone who is thirsting for revenge after many years of dependence—and are afraid of us.—
Friedrich Neitzsche, The Dawn of Morning

Preface

This book has been written as the result of a psychoanalytical as well as an astrological practice and is for use in both the astrological and psychoanalytical professions. Its method is synthetical rather than analytical as it is intended to build a bridge between two different areas of science.

Astrology is a science and, like the x-ray, it throws light onto many things that otherwise would remain hidden. My concern in the present work is primarily research into the nature of personality and character and the search for the possibility of an objective formulation of an individual's psychic orientation. I suggest this can be realized by a scientific application of astrology.

Astrology specifically employs the horoscope of the nativity. I consider it unnecessary to satisfy by argument here that demand for explanation through cause-and-effect relationships which is required by the natural scientist or even the psychologist, or to enter into a discussion of whether the moment of birth is to be taken rather than that of conception—the latter being for the most part quite unascertainable. Also incidental is the question of how the influence of the planets actually operates. The fact is, the so-called "critics" refuse to examine the factual material in any case, and the quite valid and certain science of astrology is almost completely unknown to its attackers. Whoever has really studied and understood astrology always feels positive towards it, and one can only, like Newton, say to its detractors: "I have studied the subject; you have not!" Objections are theoretical and it is—or should be—practice which decides.

As a psychoanalyst my aim is to create a bridge between psychoanalysis and astrology: to make psychoanalysis useful to astrology, and even more, to make astrology useful to psychoanalysis. Each can supplement the other, for of course astrology does have its limitations. The great French astrologer Henri Selva wrote:

> It is quite clear that one and the same astral factor, when combined with different terrestrial factors, must produce different results; the astral factor is already complex enough—the terrestrial is even more so. Therefore combinations of an almost endless variety result.

Among the many possible factors the most important are biological environment (heredity of the species, the race, the family); physical environment (climate, residence, etc.); family environment; professional, social, ethnic, political and national environment, etc. Although the knowledge of the terrestrial factors is extensive, there are nevertheless several among them which presently remain inaccessible, namely those for which the specific sciences researching them—such as psychology and sociology—have not yet attained sufficient understanding, much less precision. The result of the influence of the terrestrial factor can therefore be taken in only the crudest way as a probability through which the characteristic probabilities of the astral factors may be confirmed, strengthened or weakened. The influences under consideration here form, as it were, a hierarchy in which the astral factor assumes first place so that the astral probabilities will prevail.

That this work is concerned with homosexuality is dictated in part by the fact that it represents an area for which the sciences of today "have not attained sufficient understanding, much less precision." The assertions of Magnus Hirschfeld, for example, are nonsense in my opinion; my conception of the problem is not the general psychoanalytic one, but instead comes closer to the theories of W. S. Stekel, despite the fact that even these are not consistently worked out. But more of this in the first chapter.

First, a few explanations and remarks concerning the astrological terms used.

The Sun describes in the heavens a path called the ecliptic, which extends in an apparent leftward direction. The ecliptic and the celestial equator lie at an oblique angle to each other, and their intersecting points are the equinoxes of approximately March 21 and September 23. On the ecliptic lie the zodiac signs—each with thirty degrees and extending leftwards from the vernal equinox located at 0° Aries. The constellations of astronomy are no longer identical with the astrological signs as a result of the precession of the earth's axis among the fixed stars. It is also significant that the influence of the astrological signs of the zodiac is apparently in no way connected with the corresponding constellations of the same name, and at the present time the vernal equinox lies not near 1° Aries but rather at 8° Pisces. Perhaps it is a matter of fields of force which become effective when planets are contained therein, and the constellations may have been named after these fields, not the other way around. (The same may be true for the names of the planets.) The meanings of these zodiac signs are then in fact empirical and based upon their effects on human beings, with the result that human responses and characteristics were the basis for the names given to the zodiac signs and the constellations. This would explain the resemblance of the zodiac signs between the Indian, Egyptian, and the Chinese or Japanese zodiacs. The ethnographic factor is interesting here, and the idea that the grouping of the stars in a constellation—excepting perhaps that of Orion—represents a symbolic basis for its actual name is an erroneous notion that can nevertheless be found in as good an authority as A. Drew's *The Stars in the Poetry and Religion of Ancient Peoples and of Christianity—an Introduction to Astral Mythology.*

Within the twelve signs of the zodiac certain similarities become apparent. This gives rise to the concept of the four elements fire, earth, air, and water, which form the basis of the four fundamental kinds of temperament. In addition, there is a three-part division according to the different dynamics or rhythms of the twelve signs and known as cardinal, fixed, or mutable.

Each zodiac sign has a planet whose nature best corresponds to it and is therefore able to develop its own greatest effectiveness when located in that sign. Such a planet in this case is said to be in domicile; it is the ruler of this sign.

The twelve signs with their symbols and names, the date of the Sun's entrance into the sign, and the sign's element, rhythm and ruling planet are listed below:

1. ♈ Aries, March 21, fire, cardinal, Mars
2. ♉ Taurus, April 21, earth, fixed, Venus
3. ♊ Gemini, May 21, air, mutable, Mercury
4. ♋ Cancer, June 21, water, cardinal, Moon
5. ♌ Leo, July 22, fire, fixed, Sun
6. ♍ Virgo, August 22, earth, mutable, Mercury
7. ♎ Libra, September 23, air, cardinal, Venus
8. ♏ Scorpio, October 23, water, fixed, Mars
9. ♐ Sagittarius, November 22, fire, mutable, Jupiter
10. ♑ Capricorn, December 21, earth, cardinal, Saturn
11. ♒ Aquarius, January 20, air, fixed, Saturn, Uranus
12. ♓ Pisces, February 19, water, mutable, Jupiter, Neptune

The action of the planets is dependent upon their position in the zodiac signs. Therefore, the planets do not work unconditionally, but rather play the role of catalysts within the "fields of force" described above. In addition, their action is influenced by the aspects they form with the other planets. The cosmic state of a planet is therefore to be evaluated differently, depending on whether that planet is located in a sign where it is ruler and dominant, or in detriment or exile (the sign opposite the one which it rules), or in exaltation or fall, or is simply peregrine (with neither dignity nor debility). These and other basic qualities are now given for the planets:

The Sun is a fire planet and rules Leo, is exalted in Aries and relatively weak in Aquarius and Libra; it harmonizes with Jupiter.

The Moon rules Cancer, is exalted in Taurus, in exile or detriment in Capricorn and in fall in Scorpio; it harmonizes with Venus.

Venus rules Libra and Taurus, is in exile in Aries and Scorpio, is exalted in Pisces and in fall in Virgo; it harmonizes with Jupiter and the Moon.

Mars is in domicile in Aries and Scorpio, is in exile in Libra and Taurus, is exalted in Capricorn and in fall in Cancer; it is antagonistic to the Moon and Venus.

Jupiter rules Sagittarius and Pisces, is in exile in Gemini and Virgo, is exalted in Cancer and in fall in Capricorn; it harmonizes with the Sun and Venus.

Mercury is considered masculine as ruler of Gemini and feminine as ruler of Virgo; it is exiled in Pisces and Sagittarius.

Saturn rules Capricorn and Aquarius, is in exile in Cancer and Leo, is exalted in Libra and in fall in Aries; it is antagonistic to the Moon and Venus as well as to the Sun and Mars.

Uranus, like Neptune, does not fit into the ancient scheme of the seven visible planets, but is generally considered to be co-ruler of Aquarius. In my opinion, however, it is by no means exiled in Leo nor in fall in Taurus; it is considered to be exalted in Scorpio.

Neptune is considered to be co-ruler of Pisces.

It is significant for the quality of a planet's action whether it is moving in apparent backward motion, or retrograde.

The cosmic state is of very great importance for the effect of the aspects, and these are generally considered to be favorable or unfavorable depending on their basic harmony or disharmony. A conjunction (☌—planets in the same degree) or a trine (△—in the same degree in two signs of the same element) are harmonious in comparison with the opposition (☍—180 degrees), the square (□—90 degrees), and the semi-square (∠—45 degrees). Other aspects are the sextile (✶—60 degrees,), the semi-sextile (⊻—30 degrees), the sesquiquadrate (⬐—135 or 225 degrees), and the quincunx (⚻—150 or 210 degrees). In relationship to their aspects the planets have a certain area of valid influence surrounding them known as the orb. In judging the aspects it is important—along with the determination of the planet's cosmic state—whether the aspect is applying or separating; that is, whether the quicker of the two planets is drawing near the exact or partile aspect or whether it is already separating from it. Also the rapidity of the planet's motion or its possible retrograde motion is not without some meaning. The essential nature of the planets is therefore dependent on their position in the zodiac—their cosmic state—and also on their relationship to each other; their significance, however, is dependent on their position within and with respect to the houses.

These houses are calculated by ascertaining the degree of the zodiac passing over the local meridian at the birthtime. This degree is called the Midheaven (MC) or Medium Coeli and forms the basis of an axis vertical to that formed by the Ascendant-Descendant, which is in turn dependent on the point of sunrise on the horizon at the local latitude. By dividing the resulting quadrants by three we obtain the twelve houses through which the specific meanings of the planets become evident; this situation by house is frequently called their local determination.

The meanings of the twelve houses—not to be confused with the zodiac signs or fields of force—are given below:

First house (Ascendant or east point): the general type, personal attitude, the mission or problem in life, the destiny, the ego.

Second house: finances, substance, *desires.*

Third house: brothers and sisters, intimate acquaintances, *practical intelligence.*

Fourth house (also IC or north point): parents, foundation, the *home.*

Fifth house: love, children, pleasures, sex, creative work, *beginning.*

Sixth house: illness, servitude, duty, *giving.*

Seventh house (Descendant or west point): marriage, unions, partnerships, open enemies, complement, surrender, the *alter.*

Eighth house the non-material, mysticism, *death.*

Ninth house: higher intellect, spirituality, philosophy, long journeys, foreign countries, *knowledge.*

Tenth house (also MC or south point): profession, position, the *world.*

Eleventh house: friendship, societies, eros, *completion.*

Twelfth house: secret enemies, weaknesses, sacrifice, suffering, *renunciation.*

The houses also group themselves as follows: The first, tenth, seventh, and fourth form the quadrangle of progress; the second, eleventh, eighth, and fifth form the quadrangle of material conditions and achievements; the third, twelfth, ninth, and sixth that of silence or the mind. Moreover, the first, fifth, and ninth form the triangle of life; the tenth, second, sixth the triangle of activity (success, profit, service); the seventh, eleventh, and third form the triangle of social connections; and finally the fourth, eighth, and twelfth form the triangle of finality (heredity, suffering, dissolution).

One should always beware of schematism. For this reason I quote here a statement of Morinus:

> It is incorrect to say that the houses of a horoscope

"signify" the affairs which are attributed to them; rather they determine the influence of the planets and signs located in them. To be more precise, one ought not to say that the first house signifies life, and so forth, or the second the possessions, for it would be better to say that the first house brings about a determination which relates to life, and for that reason it is the house of life, etc. Of course, the same idea holds true for all the other houses. In the same way, the signs do not "signify" in the narrow sense of the word the affairs attributed to the houses when they are located in those houses, nor do the planets located in those houses or ruling over them, since they would then have to realize at a point in time that which they signify. To be consistent one must therefore say that the planets located in the first house contain some relative significance for life; and the same idea holds true for the remaining houses. Therefore, the location or rulership of a planet in a particular house simply gives us the information that it stands in relation to the affairs ascribed to this house. What prospects this relationship has—whether it will first bring them to pass and then cause them to be removed—is to be seen from the cosmic state of the particular planet.

Therefore the planets produce an effect dependent upon their cosmic state, their essential nature, and their relationship to the houses through their actual location therein or rulership over the houses—that is, when the sign which a planet rules falls over the cusp of a house and that planet is then said to be ruler of the house, and finally through their aspects. These things as well as the general significators, and in some cases the dispositors (for a planet in a sign other than where it is ruler becomes dependent on the ruler of this other sign) must also be carefully considered.

Chapter 1

THE PHYSICAL CONSTITUTION

In the field of psychology it was psychoanalysis that succeeded experimental psychology without, however, completely replacing it; at any rate new regions for exploration were opened up to psychology. But it was Kretschmer's work, and in particular its presentation by Kraepelin, that appeared to open up new dimensions within the field of psychiatry by postulating a relationship between psychiatric peculiarities as well as more "normal" character traits and the type of physical build or "constitution." Others, such as P. Schilder, attempted to establish relationships between psychoanalysis and physiology.

In psychiatry certainty of knowledge is not particularly notable. One knows, for example, that in paranoia a mechanism is operative where the variations are more qualitative, or that some cases of schizophrenia with catatonic stupor and dementia can come to an end; on the other hand one knows that in circular insanity (the term is used to denote all manic-depressive types in the widest sense of the words) the variations are more quantitative, and not only free intervals but even complete and lasting recovery can result. Nor is it surprising that the differences between psychosis and neurosis do not appear to be great, and that when considering neuroses, questions arise that are similar to those for psychoses; for example, the unexplained factor of organ-choice in neurosis, as well as the origin of perversions and not just their conditionality.

Even a psychoanalysis that goes back to the pregenital phases of development reveals its limits when the hypothetical assertion is made that a particular "phase" or a particular predominance of some physical zone had in fact been determinative. As a psychoanalyst I am of the unorthodox opinion that no specific zone erogeneity has an influence on the formation of character, and I consider that the component instincts have only a diagnostic importance. More significant are the so-called "complexes"—using here intentionally a word that is already somewhat outmoded; these are earlier in time and more fundamental. And even they have found expression in an overemphasis on certain phases or zones and specific zone erogeneity. Biological or physiological considerations ought to serve as a goal for psychoanalysis, and both psychology and psychiatry should try to include the factor of the physical constitution. But I do consider any attempt to evaluate types or kinds of reactions, choice of desired objectives, etc., on the basis of the physical constitution as doomed to fail, and I intend to show in this book and its case histories that such conclusions cannot be anticipated from research into the physical constitution.

The connection between physical constitution and character is not nearly so close as was earlier assumed. The organization of character and personality I designate as the *constellation*. I use this term in a sense that is similar to the concept of the physical constitution *and* condition; that is, similar to a concept descriptive of an actual state and including past and present conditioning factors. I will add that just as the entire physical condition depends on the physiological features which become fixed in and at birth, so also it is my opinion that all the characterological features—including the so-called complexes—are in fact fixed at birth also, and the image of this reality is the *constellation* I have

The Physical Constitution

mentioned. Its mechanisms and to some extent its destiny can be ascertained.

First I want to prove the existence of such a *character-constellation* and that it is independent of the physical constitution. Furthermore, in chapter 3 I will show the precise necessity of introducing such a concept as well as show the possibility of ascertaining it and with astrological means.

But I wish to begin with some remarks about the constitution as it was presented by Kretschmer. This author shows in his *Physique and Character* how the features of manic-depressive circular insanity on the one hand and paranoia and schizophrenia on the other correspond to a duality within the normal personality. These are the cyclothymic and the schizothymic individuals. Kretschmer also described the types of physique which showed certain affinities to both these psychiatric as well as personality types.

The first physical type Kretschmer describes is the *asthenic* or *leptosomic* type: thin, lean, tall, little body fat, long narrow breastcage, narrow shoulders, long limbs with thin musculature, narrow-jointed fingers, an oval front-face and angular profile. Kretschmer's second type is the *athletic*: average or medium tall in height, broad shoulders, developed breastcage, strong limbs, the lower jaw is roundish but well-developed. The third type is the *pyknic*: medium-size, compact, barrel-shaped body, but the limbs are lighter and less developed; a short, drawn-in neck that inclines forward; the face is shield-shaped or pentagonal; sometimes bald. The remainder are relegated to a fourth group, the *dysplastics*—a classification which seems to me to be not entirely suitable. Almost half of these are tall, heavy-set, eunuch types, an extreme variant of the asthenic type which are partly characterized by infantile, asexual, dysgenital traits. Only the remaining hypoplastic and polyglandular obese types should in my opinion be considered as dysplastic, for any relatedness these have to the schizophrenia group is very doubtful.

With respect to constitution, then, the schizophrenic and the schizothymic belong for the most part to the asthenic, less often to the athletic, seldom to the dysplastic group as defined by Kretschmer, and very seldom to the pyknic. Kretschmer found the highest relationship to schizophrenia among the leptosomes, while on the other hand the asthenic, leptosomic, athletic, and dysplastic as well as their mixed types show the least connection to the circular form of mental illness as well as the cyclothymic character. Further, the greatest *affinity* to circular psychoses and the cyclothymic character is found among the roundish pyknic types.

So, the schizothymic character group is distinguished physically from the barrel-shaped roundish form of the pyknic physique, as well as from the cyclothymic character associated with the pyknic type—comfort-loving, sociable, friendly, at times warmly humorous but also at times quiet and serious.

Naturally, combinations of physique types appear when the character types are themselves found in combination, but the schizothymic character, corresponding to the asthenic or leptosomic physique type, displays specific character traits which stand in contrast to those other humans who are normally talkative, cheerful, humorous, quietly emotional, comfort-loving enjoyers of life and active as well as practical. Instead, the schizothymic character oscillates between sensitivity and coldness, and the lack of middle areas of affective response is one of its most striking features.

Kretschmer describes schizothymic characters as those who are exalted in attitude—the impractical idealists, the cold dominating natures and egoists—all opposed to the pyknic "enjoyer." Among writers and poets he makes a distinction between the romantics, the writers of tragedy, the artists of form, and the pyknic realists and humorists; among scientists a distinction between the logician, the systematic thinker, the metaphysician, and the pyknic who tends to vivid descriptions of reality and experience; among leaders a distinction between the pure idealists, the despots, the fanatics, and the pyknics who are rather crude go-getters, active organizers or intelligent mediators.

So while the pyknics and the cycloids are for the most part straightforward, humorous, and uncomplicated, the schizothymics are absorbed by what is complicated and problematic. Of these Kretschmer says:

> They are cutting, brutal or sullen, dull or stinging, ironic or hypershy, withdrawn as if without protection—that at any rate is the surface. Or the surface tells nothing at all, and we see before us a person who is a question mark yet we sense something flat, tedious, but ambiguous. What is it that lies beneath all these masks? It may be nothing, and behind a silent facade where moods at best flicker and are stifled nothing exists except rubble, black ruins, vacant emotions, or the coldest lack of heart. But we cannot see what is behind the face, and many schizoid persons are like cold Roman houses—villas that have closed their shutters before the glaring sun while within the darkened light inside hold great festivities.

These features manifest themselves in other ways, and particular types include the tragic or romantic individuals, as well as the idealistic and revolutionary. Their artistic expression is lyric or tragic, and there is generally an almost constant mental conflict; perhaps they even have a personal disposition or talent for what is tragic. Kretschmer also states that the idyllic and the heroic are schizothymic complementary moods.

The outstanding individual or personal manifestation is that of the aristocrat with greatness of mind, tenacity in adverse circumstances, severity, purity and integrity of the personal style. In other words the style of life is heroic.

Character traits result in a life style that is for the most part markedly aristocratic, such as the tendency to select a society or an exclusive circle where there is a de-emphasis of all affective elements in personal intercourse—an "extended autism among the like-minded"—apart from the common people "where there is an ecstatic cult of personality outside of which all common people are avoided and despised." Kretschmer continues: "The schizoid does not go out into the environment; the 'pane of glass' is always there." Among hyper-esthetic types there frequently develops a sharp awareness of ego versus the rest of the world. "These are people who have constant mental conflict and whose life is lived as a chain of tragedies or as a long thorny path of suffering. They have, if one may say so, a natural talent for the tragic. Altruistic self-sacrifice in the grand manner, particularly for general or impersonal ideals, is quite characteristic."

For the schizothymic philosopher or thinker there results a lack of ability to popularize, a lack of broad general understanding coupled with the maintenance of egoistic viewpoints. The minds of rulers, for example, are seldom free from schizothymic traits, but this does not prevent Kretschmer from finding many highly gifted individuals among the pyknic. In contrast to the pyknic tendency to graphic description, Kretschmer finds primarily leptosomes and schizothymes among those who lean to exact theories such as religious mystics, precise logicians and systematic thinkers, and among writers those who are much concerned with formal style, as well as the romantic metaphysicians who are concerned with feelings. "The ones inclined to tragedy or pathos have the more temperamental and instinct-prone natures, while the romantics are more psychasthenic types—tender, feminine—those who are in flight from the world. Tragic pathos is the battle of the autistic mind against reality, elegiac romanticism is its flight from it."

Along with a capacity for delicate expression and hypersensitivity there is found a humorless seriousness with no clear expression of grief or gladness. Kretschmer says: "They are often ill-tempered, but this ill-humor is something quite different from the sadness of the cycloid, and is rather an inner nervous

The Physical Constitution

irritability. This is why one can find among the schizoids such constitutionally ill-tempered persons who go on restless journeys while the inhibitory depression remains always with them."

The tendency to all-or-nothing is also expressed in their love life. Kretschmer says: "Not warm affection for them, but either ecstasy or a harsh coldness. They do not search for a pretty girl but for the Absolute Woman. They are either saints or shrews and there is no in-between."

We shall now review the general features of schizophrenic thought so that we may recognize that it bears a very close relationship to artistic creativity, particularly writing. This is even more true for the creative intuition of real genius. One observation to be made is that from the search for the "Absolute Woman" rather than just "a pretty girl" arises the phenomenon of polygamy rather than monogamy, and polygamy is typically masculine. (F. Boehm has even stated—in my opinion somewhat exaggeratedly—that the degree of polygamy corresponds to the degree of homosexuality determined and determinable by psychoanalysis.) Further, genius is per se typically masculine, and the pyknics are-according to one observer-capable of only very good talent. In any case, we wish definitively to propose that certain relationships exist between schizophrenia and schizothymia on the one hand and formal artistry, poetic genius, polygamy and masculinity on the other.

It is interesting that Kretschmer emphasized that errors occur during self-diagnosis so that the schizothymic individual has a tendency to take himself for a cyclothymic.

As the particular area of interest in this work is homosexuality, we note that Kretschmer has already asserted that they are "of more uncertain drives." And the fact that homosexuality in its essence and type belongs to the schizothymic group will be shown more clearly further on. It is interesting to note here that the fact homosexuals belong to the schizothymic leptosomes makes it more understandable why earlier "scientific opinions" believed to be able to identify the homosexual as a typical "degenere superieur" and described him as a tall, thin, decadent, aristocratic individual.

It also ought to be mentioned here that no connection exists between the constitution types described by Kretschmer and the different racial types, and this is not unimportant for my thesis. On the other hand, some writers have observed a certain affinity, for example, between the northern European and the schizothymic-asthenic type.

I would like to quote several passages from astrological literature in order to draw certain parallels with Kretschmer's ideas and I have chosen for this Oscar A. H. Schmitz's *The Spirit of Astrology* published in Munich in 1916. While Schmitz's book can be considered as only an introduction to astrology, his intuitive descriptions of the signs are the best presentations I know of, and I quote these in order to protect myself from the unfair charge that any interpretations of my own would be tailored to prove my own arguments.

The leptosome type is found, on a perusal of any astrological writings, to be described again and again in connection with the influence of the zodiac sign Aquarius. Schmitz states that this type may possess "beauty of an intellectual or spiritual kind; long face, deep, enigmatic eyes; long finely shaped chin."

Characteristic is the Aquarian's mental freedom, far from any connection with subjective emotions. "He is much more the one who has gone through the sin of matter and through the knowledge of good and evil to become himself like the gods." Further, they are

> . . . amiable, happy, and despite their love for solitude in no way unsociable, but instead excellent friends-only, however, towards a few on whom they have the greatest psychic influence. They show a just and kindly attitude for all humanity over which they

frequently find themselves elevated. In spite of the considerable fascination they often exert they see too deeply to please the many and they are never popular as they seem somewhat uncanny to most and are seldom understood. They have little value in the market place, but exclusive circles are often easily accessible to them while they instinctively avoid those that anyone may enter. Their lack of illusions frightens some and is taken for cynicism, and in all human endeavor they constantly see the opposite point of view and through this they recognize that any human wish formulated into a program will be unjust.

When Aquarius reaches his fullest development he then becomes "the master of his fate, which cannot longer affect him, and is experienced as a mirror of his own inner being seen from the outside. The sculptor can again be optimistic because he knows himself as a creative middlepoint and considers himself stronger than the pessimistically perceived world." It is interesting that according to Schmitz, Venus in Aquarius makes the appearance feminine-an incorrect statement in our opinion which is not, however, surprising since, if "youthful" is itself frequently and erroneously designated as "feminine," why not a refined appearance as well? It seems significant that the ancient Greeks also knew Aquarius as the constellation of Ganymede.

As was stated in the preface Aquarius is the domicile of Saturn, known also as the "greater malefic." But also, Uranus is considered to rule Aquarius. Mars, on the other hand, is sometimes known as the "lesser malefic" and has its domicile in Scorpio, where Uranus is also considered to be exalted.

The external appearance of the sign Scorpio is described by Schmitz: "For the most part strong, of middle height, square-build and large-boned, the legs are often too short or misshapen. Frequently there is a birthmark that has little color; the chin and jaw are bony, angular and wide. The tightly compressed lips express a conscious reserve." One must therefore assume dysplastic traits are mixed in, but I have also recognized a Scorpio type with compact, athletic legs, massive, almost pyknic lower body, extended trunk—so that they sit quite tall but with sharply sloping shoulders and a long neck; in other words, they are asthenic from the breastline upwards. There is also a recognizable type which is similar to the popular notion of the physical appearance associated with the devil, and this strikes me as remarkably intuitive when one realizes that the genital area is attributed to this sign and that among neurotics sexuality is frequently seen as "devilish." Interesting also is the fact that at one time the symbol for this sign in Egypt was the serpent. Schmitz goes on to say:

> Scorpio is the domicile of Mars, who must descend into matter in order to give to it the stamp of individuation, to make himself felt in each separate creature. It is the sign of the two extremes good and evil. Its action is typical of the strongest individualism and of all individualistic realizations, while its purpose is power over matter, and its tendency is to "all or nothing."
>
> Their road to knowledge begins with a sense curiosity which tastes and samples matter. The lowest sensuality as well as ascetic self-control; wallowing in a subhuman state as well as a rising to the super-human; cynical lack of honor as well as unshakable self-assurance; crass materialism and the highest mysticism-all these contrasts are Scorpionic and in fact they always appear with the greatest decisiveness. It is not only the sign of mysticism but of magic, both black and white. Unlike the other mystical sign Pisces—where there is so much self-deception—there is here no such thing. Scorpio may deceive others, but never itself. Here we find the fanatics and martyrs who are ready to mount the pyre for all or for nothing, but when they sacrifice themselves it is done in a sense of separation or discrimination. When, however, Scorpio is an atheist or

The Physical Constitution

an enemy of religion he is such with the same inner fire of the religious fanatic. His leadership, in contrast to that of Aries-the masculine domicile of Mars—is less visible, and he often is found controlling things from behind the scenes. His courage is of passive self-assurance rather than actively aggressive. He has nothing at all of the blind courage of the dare-devil, but rather the knowing courage of one who while seeing the danger feels confident that he can overcome it. [Therefore, the leader who is the "exact calculator" as Kretschmer describes it among the possibilities of the schizothymic type.] Almost always there is something mysterious about him. Even on a relatively low intellectual level he makes sharp distinctions, chooses words according to their original sense and can with one blow cut through errors, misunderstandings, and ambiguities, while at the same time when he chooses he can himself be a master of ambiguity. His mind is therefore a paradox.

I now quote Schmitz's description of two zodiac types, of which the first—Gemini—is markedly leptosomic ("tall, thin, active") and the second—Sagittarius—is a combination leptosomic-athletic type ("large, frequently good-looking, good but somewhat corpulent build, strong nose, high forehead, sharp eyes, noble expression"). I do not quote here Schmitz's descriptions of the athletic types Aries and Leo.

In Gemini, Mercury is masculine and is the ruler of this sign.

In contrast with the characters of Aquarius and Scorpio, which are recognizable by the antitheses of their double nature, Gemini is unrestrained in its double nature. This type is restless, impatient, lacking in concentration, busy, but also idealistic and very often superficially happy; witty and refined, but also talkative, nervous, excitable, unself-contained, and seldom persistent. [Their intelligence, in contrast to Scorpio, tends to be average.] Gemini is completely unbelieving-he believes neither in that which is holy nor that which is vile. That which is human interests him but not in the sense that what is human embodies values. He swears on what is human and does not want, as does Scorpio, to "be like God—knowing good and evil." The typical Gemini type is unredeemable because the human—and in particular a developed intellect—is for him an end-in-itself. The world of ideas of a typical Gemini is like a film; it can connect numerous impressions and thoughts one after the other, but never two at the same time, and he therefore knows an endless amount of things but perceives nothing, as do Scorpio and Aquarius by the antitheses of their natures. For this reason he has no ongoing development, only endless variations. The inexpressible and the mysterious hold nothing for him.

His character is "very actively interested and intelligent, but without any warmth; he is neither passionate and carried-away, nor wise and detached." He is supremely intellectual and takes that for spiritual. His interest lands immediately on something when it is thought over and its nature reduced to a formula. His ambition is more restless than intense. He is completely unhistorical and without piety.

He who everywhere mediates relations is himself at bottom without relations. As a result of his superficiality he cannot be alone, and must be able to talk to someone—be it foolishness, and he must have relationships—be they bad ones. No one is less exclusive and that, he feels, is his humanity. He picks things up without selectivity for he does not want to work through anything, but only find out what goes on around him. He does not understand what the self is and recognizes only the ego. Wit means almost everything to him. He

The Physical Constitution

seldom remains at the task, but shines in many colors and makes appearance in many professions. He gladly avoids difficulties, and easily lets a task go unfinished.

Schmitz says the following regarding the typical Sagittarius:

> Sagittarius makes seers, prophets, leaders of every kind; and at a lower level those individuals who do not carry in Saturnine fashion the curse of matter and wearily try to extricate themselves from it, but instead conquer it without effort [for example, as athletes]. Principal characteristics of Sagittarius are liveliness, impulsiveness, ambition, passion, independence, sense of justice, mental and physical activity, tendency to over-exertion, good-naturedness, reliability and sympathy. They do not endure confined circumstances and they love wide-open places. Their danger is much more likely to be superstition than a scientific positivism bound to the exact facts and based on utility.

The connection between the schizothymic character and the leptosomic physique is closer than between the schizothymic character and the athletic physique. Kretschmer does not emphasize this but it can be concluded from his book. In a table (no. 5) he gives the classification according to physique for 175 schizophrenics: 81 asthenics, 31 athletics, 11 asthenic-athletic mixed types, 34 dysplastics, 13 deformed and therefore unclassifiable, 5 (!!) pyknics, as well as their mixed types.

A consideration of these astrological passages shows that the connection between schizothymic character and the leptosomic physique is particularly striking among Aquarius and Gemini types, and to some extent among Scorpio types, including the type described by myself where the lower body is athletic, the trunk is large, and the upper part of the body is asthenic. Athletic features were to some extent in evidence among Sagittarius types. The signs Aries and Leo are of an almost pure athletic type and masculine—Aries because of its heightened activity and Leo because of its greater vitality. The point is that among these latter one finds fewer schizothymic traits. In any case, affinity between schizothymia and the leptosomic physique can be traced through astrology as can an affinity to the athletic types, while the sign Scorpio represents a combination of types and is therefore "dysplastic" in nature.

We have also stated that the ruler of Aquarius is Saturn or Uranus, of Scorpio Mars, of Gemini the masculine Mercury, and of Sagittarius Jupiter; these planetary rulers are all masculine, as are the rulers of the "athletic" signs Aries and Leo—i.e. Mars and the Sun respectively.

The twelve zodiac types are now given here in terms of their physique and character in Kretschmer's terms.

Aries: athletic physique, asthenic traits, virile character with schizothymic traits.

Taurus: pyknic physique, phlegmatic and cyclothymic character.

Gemini: asthenic physique, schizothymic character.

Cancer: a lymphatic and pyknic physique; passive, cyclothymic character.

Leo: athletic physique; vital, schizothymic character.

Virgo: a pyknic mixed type; mixed character type-cyclic, but also schizothymic.

Libra: mixed type, balanced character.

Scorpio: mixed type with dysplastic traits; schizothymic character.

Sagittarius: asthenic-athletic physique; schizothymic character.

Capricorn: mixed type with dysplastic traits; a rather schizothymic character.

Aquarius: asthenic physique; schizothymic character.

Pisces: lymphatic, pyknic type; receptive, cyclothymic character.

This classification applies to men only, which will by nature incline it towards a schizothymic character.

When I calculate the zodiac types by percentage according to their physique types, I obtain approximately 17 percent asthenic, 8 percent asthenic-athletic, 17 percent athletic, 17 percent mixed types with dysplastic traits, 8 percent mixed types, 8 percent mixed pyknic types, and 25 percent pyknics.

The types according to Kretschmer as well as my figures here refer only to men. Kretschmer states that the feminine constitution appears in more "blurred and mixed forms. These are found among both men and women, but because of the generally lesser differentiation of the female body the extreme traits appear more seldom among women."

Classical astrology goes on to break down the twelve zodiac types into three-fold and four-fold groups. The elements—as matter—correspond to a breakdown by four, while a "spiritual" breakdown corresponds, as always, to the number three. The four elements, which already have been described in the preface, correspond to the four humors as understood by the ancients and are based on a concept of constitution (!):

The choleric, corresponding to the element fire, includes Aries, Leo and Sagittarius, and the principal humor of yellow bile.

The phlegmatic, corresponding to the earth, includes Taurus, Virgo and Capricorn, and the principal humor of black bile of the venous blood.

The melancholic, corresponding to water, includes Cancer, Scorpio and Pisces, and the principal humor of mucus and lymph.

The sanguine, corresponding to the element air (since it was considered that in a corpse the bloodless arteries were filled with air), includes Gemini, Aquarius, and Libra.

By contrast there is the division by four, corresponding to

the Indian gunas, and in each of the three crosses or quadrangles each of the four elements appears, so that from this the twelve-count of the zodiac is built up. The quadrangles or crosses have already been given as cardinal—Aries F, Cancer W, Libra A, and Capricorn E; fixed-Taurus E, Leo F, Scorpio W, Aquarius A; and finally the common signs—Gemini A, Virgo E, Sagittarius F, Pisces W. The cardinal signs also correspond to a factor of mentality, the fixed to one of vitality and the common to one of motion. It is notable that even Kretschmer, without any knowledge of these concepts, sensed their divisions and made a difference between the constitutional "temperament" and the psychic rhythm or motility—the latter corresponding to the quadrangles above.

As our material refers to males, the normal two-fold division into masculine and feminine signs will be taken here rather as a division between the mixed-form types corresponding to the earth and water signs and the asthenic-athletic types corresponding to the air and fire signs. Such a division is nothing new, and Aries, Gemini, Leo, Libra, Sagittarius and Aquarius were considered even in antiquity to be positive or masculine in contrast to the negative or feminine signs Taurus, Cancer, Virgo, Scorpio, Capricorn, and Pisces.

This brings us to a significant formulation: The athletic-leptosomic constitution, the basic temperament of fire-air—that is, choleric and sanguine—and the schizothymic character are masculine criteria, while the pyknic-lymphatic constitution, the basic temperament of earth-water—that is, phlegmatic and melancholic—and the cyclothymic character are feminine criteria.

The possibilities that result here are very considerable, but there must first be some proof of the formula given. It goes without saying that there should therefore be a greater affinity of men to schizophrenia and a correspondingly greater affinity of women to the circular psychoses.

Again there is not much statistical data, but one finds, for example in the textbooks on psychiatry by Stransky or by Pilz, the statement that varieties of melancholia and mania are more frequently found among women and are more typical of them.

Also it is clear how different a psychosis is with, for example, progressive paralysis, in its unmistakable relation to the physical constitution, and the features are clearly more schizoid. And this is true in general for the kinds of manifestations of progressive paralysis-psychosis among men and among women. And finally, there is the common experience in madhouses of how striking the difference is between the wards for men and women—there is much greater unrest and noisiness among the women.

In Kretschmer's divisions by constitution there is a significant contrast between the athletic or asthenic types, where the formation of the head and musculature are more prominent as well as identified with masculinity, and the pyknic type where the emphasis is on the development of the trunk and more receptive feelings, which are identified with femininity. It is understood that among men the specific characteristics are manifested in a tendency to the development of the trunk. A third type is non-sexual and tall, but this is at the same time an adolescent type.

Kretschmer emphasized that pure types are unusual, and the same must be taken into account in judging astrological types; physique types are not absolutes, but combinations occur with a relative emphasis moving in one direction or the other. Even in the most masculine athletic-asthenic-schizothymic group the feminine cyclothymic can be found. Bleuler was also of this opinion, and it concurs with the theory of Fliess that all persons are both masculine and feminine because of the conditions of their evolution.

It seems important that in both the work done in the last five years by Kretschmer's followers such as Gruhl and H. Krisch, as well as his strongest opponents such as K. Kolle, the relationships of the pyknic type to circular insanity has been established beyond any objection, and among men the pyknic type is to be regarded as a type approaching the characteristics of the opposite sex. A similar idea is found in the work of Swoboda and W. Fliess, who propose a concept of periodicity according to which the twenty-eight day lunar cycle plays a role among women, while a cycle of twenty-three days described by Fliess is significant for men. (Wilhelm Fliess was a nose and throat specialist in Berlin at the turn of the century whose interests extended far beyond his specialization. He was a friend of Freud and operated on him on two occasions. He became president of the German Academy of Sciences in 1910. His studies on bisexuality resulted in his theory of the twenty-eight and twenty-three day cycles which he considered to appear simultaneously in both sexes. *Hermann Swoboda* was professor of psychiatry at the University of Vienna during the same time and developed a theory of periodicity in psychological fluctuations which were based on the individual's *birthdate*—see his *The Critical Days of Man*, Vienna, 1909. These theories formed the basis of the current studies in biorhythm—see the best-selling *Is This Your Day?* by George S. Thommen, NYC, 1973.) The cyclical concept of 28 days seems at once more significant biologically for women than for men, while the twenty-three day cycle described by Fliess for men seems to me to be questionable (twenty-three days—for what it is worth—is a fifth of the synodic period of Mercury).

The objections could be made that, for example, even among pyknic types one finds baldness and unseen angular formations, while on the other hand the angle of the temple indentations among asthenic-schizophrenic types is markedly female in character. But this is conditioned by a different factor that is characteristic of the asthenic—he is a more archaic type. This explains as well his more developed and extensive hairiness.

In the dysplastic group Kretschmer claims that a half are unusually tall, eunuchoid types, while the other half are those men and women who display intermediate characteristics, but I have observed no men of this latter type who could not be considered as pyknic, or a youthful sub-type of this group. The tall eunuchoid type tends not to the characteristics of the opposite sex but rather to asexuality. This is a specifically physical factor that also seems to be biologically and constitutionally related to race, and perhaps it forms the basis for the asexual tendency in the sexuality of the nordic racial type. If these two groups are classified otherwise, and the tall eunuchoid types are categorized as extreme leptosomic types—which is where I think almost all of the schizoids of Kretschmer's dysplastic group belong—and the other intermediate types are relegated elsewhere, I am of the opinion that this catch-all group would almost completely disappear. One sees clearly how differently these concepts have been evaluated by the variation in percentages given by different authors on the subject. But it seems logical that if one subtracts the men from the dysplastic group, most of these "intermediate" types can be ascribed to the pyknic group. In chapter 7 we will go into the problem of the female dysplastic types which are characterized by masculinity, athletic or asthenic physique traits and the schizothymic character associated with them.

It is sometimes uncertain whether the phlegmatic or melancholic types should be ascribed to the earth element or to the water element, and this seems to be explained by the difficulty in distinguishing between the phlegmatic but apparently melancholic, and the melancholic but apparently phlegmatic. Also of interest is the symbolism of the elements themselves; on a mythological basis fire, air, and the heavens are seen as masculine in psychoanalysis, while the earth (the womb of mother-earth) and water (the most well-known and common symbol of birth) are seen as feminine.

Sexuality is rooted in the nature taken as a whole—in the constitution and character, and the zodiac is significant in this respect through the distribution of planets therein at birth. It is also interesting that certain degrees of the zodiac are said to have an influence that predisposes to homosexuality, and these are 25° Leo-Aquarius and 8° Aries-Libra when the Ascendant-

Descendant or the cusps of the fifth-eleventh houses fall on these degrees, and this naturally applies to any planet which is significator of these things and falls in these degrees. Charles E. O. Carter made this observation, but my own data are not sufficient for me to pass judgment on it.

The most individualistic features result from the specific determinations of the planets, but one can obtain significant clues on the basic sexuality of the individual from the planetary distribution such as when certain signs contain a majority of the planets. For example, when there is a preponderance of planets in the fire signs, the love life will show a certain verve, energy and idealism, but planets badly placed there result in an increase in aggressiveness or the use of force. Planets well placed in the earth signs cause strong but controlled passions, while badly placed they result in a tendency to crude pleasures and a brutal and materialistic attitude. In the air signs planets well placed give refined aspirations but when badly placed the romantic instincts lose their element of feeling and become over-intellectualized. When the majority of planets, and especially the significators, are in the water signs and well placed, then in love there is a tendency to romantic notions of all kinds varying from mental dreaminess up to mystical passion, but when badly placed they result in hysteria or overexcitement of the senses, indolence and lack of resistance in sexual matters.

From the pattern of emphasis in the quadruplicities one sees the dynamism which will be combined with the particular temperament. The basic principle is that the cardinal signs are mental, the fixed are vital, and the common signs are flexible, so that in the sex life there results when planets are well placed in cardinal signs a self-assertive leadership and sustaining passion, while when badly placed a tendency to dominate, to exert undue influence, and to be seductive and insatiable. When the planets are well placed in the fixed signs a calm, worthy, true, reliable nature is found, while when badly placed the instincts are uncontrolled and vulgar. When the planets are well placed in the common signs a versatile flexibility is found, while when badly placed instability, fickleness, lack of resolution, self-will, and moodiness.

Apart from the cosmic state of the planet—that is, apart from its position in the zodiac—the most important things to note are that a particular planet is actually located in a house, is ruler of the sign on the cusp, or is in turn the dispositor of that planet or forms an important aspect with it. But the general nature of the planets themselves says something about their behavior in relation to sexuality.

The Sun is strong, vital, fiery, heating, masculine, and when well placed tends to healthy, noble passion, while when badly placed to subjugation and the use of force in sex.

The Moon is plastic, fruitful, sentimental, feminine, and when well placed brings to one's love life a breadth of feeling, sentimentality even to the point of melancholia, and gives a milder form to the expression of passion; badly placed it works in some inharmonious way dependent upon the sign in which it is placed and its dispositor.

Venus is soft, passive, and feminine, and as it has a close relationship to sex, a careful study of it is always well worthwhile.

Mars is strong, masculine, active, inflaming, unfruitful, and when well placed indicates healthy and strong passions; while badly placed he inclines to excesses, hyper-aggression, violence and a crude sexuality.

Jupiter is moderate, well-tempered, active, fruitful and masculine, and when well placed grants healthy erotic instincts which manifest themselves with agreeable passionateness, but when badly placed the planet inclines to sexual excess and to hypocrisy.

Mercury, whose sexual nature is ambivalent, is excitable, changeable, and moderately fruitful, and inclines when well placed to moderation in sensual desires, but when badly placed to moodiness, unreliability, superficiality, and instability.

Saturn—the "greater malefic"—is negative, unfruitful, obstructing, and masculine, but his influence can nevertheless be very positive. In particular, he always brings a certain depth and when well placed he sublimates passions, spiritualizes and instructs, but when badly placed he leads to unusual forms of sexual expression that cannot be considered favorable. Carter has emphasized already the perverting influence of an unfavorable Saturn.

Uranus will be considered more carefully further on; it has the strongest relationship to homosexuality and to the male eros.

Neptune represents dissolution—even when well placed—and according to the astrologer Sinbad he primarily brings spirituality and mystical longings for something higher, causes presentiments to arise, and bathes the world in an aura of the unreal. When badly placed he is hysterical, neurotic, neurasthenic and perverse, and Carter says specifically that in a sexual context he causes neurotic states, nymphomania, and compulsive attitudes towards sex. He mentions one such case where Mercury was conjunct Neptune in the 5th house and square Mars as well as trine Uranus. I have found Neptune to have the closest relationship to female homosexuality, and to psychoses as well.

In one case of a female hebephrenic the Ascendant was 9°34' Cancer, and when the Ascendant progressed to the conjunction of Neptune retrograde in the first house, the psychoses appeared. In the natal horoscope Neptune was conjunct Moon in the first house, parallel Jupiter in the sixth house and ruler of the sixth, and also sextile Saturn intercepted in Taurus in the eleventh house. Libra was on the cusp of the fifth house. The Ascendant progressed to the square of Mercury located on the cusp of the eleventh house caused the psychosis to begin, and when the Ascendant progressed 2°08' to the conjunction of the Moon—that is, one year and six days later—it was made clearly manifest.

Venus in Libra differs from its location in Taurus in that the latter position is more deeply sunk into matter and is therefore more primitive; in Libra Venus always has a more refined quality. While in Taurus it represents blind attraction, in Libra it brings a love which includes a recognition of the partner. The Venus-Taurus type is the typical female whose polar opposite is Mars in Aries.

Venus in Scorpio, the sign of its exile, is the worst sign for the planet, and of this position Schmitz says: "Here her fire is completely fettered and either she is quite frigid or capable of vice without warmth, but always corrupted by the negative qualities of Mars."

In the other two earth signs the planet is likewise unfavorably placed; in Virgo it is debilitated not only by the egoism of this sign but it takes on a markedly prudish quality, and if, in addition, "Mars aspects Venus, or Jupiter is in bad aspect to it, its nature is made lascivious while under the cover of hypocrisy." In Capricorn, Venus not only falls sway to the essential nature of Saturn, resulting in a cooling-off of erotic sentiment, but there also results—especially if it is aspected by malefic planets—an unusually low passion, calculation or dissoluteness.

In Pisces, where the planet is exalted, the favorable influence of the jupiterian nature of this sign is noticeable, but in this position and in the other water sign Cancer—which tends to unsteadiness—the capacity for sensation needs exterior stimulus for it to be awakened.

Venus in the air sign Gemini is relatively favorable, but its action in Aquarius has different possibilities. In this sign it "tends to a deep erotic activity transforming the inner life and which seeks to manifest itself in a spiritualized way," therefore inclines to eros, but also has capacities for sublimation. Finally, Venus is emphatic and direct in Leo, even more so in Sagittarius, while in Aries the planet is in detriment, and the sign makes the planet too ardent; even women are made crude under this influence.

Some consideration of the various aspects of the planet Venus is also in order. It is striking that even in the earliest astrological literature mention sometimes is made concerning the "bad" aspects of Venus (the square and the opposition) with the malefic planets Saturn or Mars and, later, with Uranus. These sweeping generalizations are erroneous, yet there is also a kernel of truth contained in them. It is not possible to say that certain aspects have an effect which is the same at all times, despite the fact that they recur more frequently in certain situations where they also have some specific influence, since everything that is really significant results from quite specific determinations. If the squares and oppositions of Mars and Saturn to Venus were always taken as indications of homosexuality, then for example, in the year 1905 all those born from June 6 to 20 (Venus opposition Saturn), July 7 to 13 (Venus square Saturn), September 21 to 28 (Venus square Mars), and December 4 to 8 (Venus square Saturn) would have to be considered homosexual. This is, of course, not the case.

It is necessary to study in greater detail the planets Uranus and Neptune. Regarding their influence one might say in general that Neptune blurs and softens to the point of chaotic indefiniteness, while Uranus is more sharp and jolting. The effect of both is for the most part destructive—confusion through Neptune, restlessness and turbulence through Uranus.

For the Neptunian type, Oscar A. H. Schmitz describes a large range of possibilities. For the most part Neptune makes one "uncertain, anxious, sickly, hypersensitive, utopian and fanatical," but he also stimulates occult influences of those otherwise known as "astral." So when well developed, he opens the door to knowledge and perception. "The life of the Neptunian seems actually to be ruled by demons: Without knowing how or why, they fall prey to every possible aberrational idea concerning deceptions, mysteries, plots, and even debauchery, scandals and crime. Serious states of anxiety as result of unknown causes, much change, unexpected gains and losses, intrigues and backbiting which at times they instigate and at times are made to endure at the hands of others; bigamy, double-lives" are all concepts that are quite typical.

The insistent claim that Neptune is ruler of Pisces does not seem to be justified, as the planet would then have to be in detriment in Virgo, just as Uranus would be in Leo if we assume that Uranus rules Aquarius. But this is not the case; Neptune and Uranus lie outside of the scheme of seven planets known to the ancients. One finds that Neptune in Virgo is unusually romantic; in the other earth signs Taurus and Capricorn his influence is less characteristic and less clear. In the fire signs his influence is by no means weakened but, on the contrary, strengthened. In Aries he is particularly enlivening, in Sagittarius revolutionary, in Leo he breaks the ground for the romanticism that follows. Neptune in the air signs is not particularly marked but is vague and sentimental, and in Libra there is a certain hermaphroditic quality in the sense of a creative balance or equilibrium. In the water signs, except for Pisces, Neptune does not appear to have any generally characteristic influence, but in Cancer there is a peculiar hypersensitivity, and in Scorpio there is mysticism. One difficulty in judging these things results from the fact that in larger epochs of time it is often difficult to separate the influence of Uranus from Neptune.

Schmitz describes the effects of Uranus as follows: "The highly developed Uranian is similar both inwardly and outwardly to the higher type of Aquarian," and "he goes beyond the boundaries of the strictly human. For him who is unable to grasp this Uranus becomes a destroyer, while for him who understands he is a savior—albeit with a heavy hand." His effects are sudden, "but these are never random episodes but turns in the course of destiny." The developed Uranian type is "rather quiet, modest, not very enthusiastic, but all this proceeds from an inner freedom which stands beyond law, morality, convention, mode and party. But before all this can come to pass the Uranian has times of whimsical eccentricity, or gets mired down in a form of pseudo-genius that shows itself in contempt of forms, which he always feels are there to persecute him. These persons band together in heretical groups as reformers of religion, education, marriage and even love itself, while in the arts they try to shock and are usually modern and bohemian in style.

In considering the effect of Uranus when placed in the different zodiac signs it ought to be noted that its effect in the air sign Aquarius is not nearly so clear as is sometimes supposed. Its general influence in Gemini is favorable, its influence in Libra is strong and important and is similar to Neptune in Libra in that it shows the same creative equilibrium. In general, the air signs are better than the earth signs for this planet. When located in the water signs, Uranus seems to be peregrine; in Pisces it is without significance, in Cancer not unfavorable, but is somewhat stronger in Scorpio. In the earth sign Taurus it is rather indecisive, in Virgo somewhat more favorable, in Capricorn there is a certain materialistic tendency, however unsteady. (During the period from 1904 to 1911 when Uranus was in Capricorn the less favorable influence of Uranus was more to be attributed to its opposition to Neptune rather than to its location in Capricorn.) The fire signs are favorable for Uranus and contribute to the planet's strongly active tendency. The very masculine characteristics of Uranus have a greater effect in the masculine signs; that is, in the fire and air signs.

Schmitz describes Uranus as "intuitive, explosive, vulcanic, energetic, maturing, self-willed, unpredictable, obstinate, intellectual, bisexual, asexual, enigmatic, heroic, creative, hypercritical, sarcastic, disorderly, perverse, flashing, paradoxical, sometimes deceptively vacuous-sometimes extremely deep." And again we emphasize that all these are schizothymic traits! "Only the highly developed individual will receive other than destructive influences from Uranus." This is particularly true in one certain respect: Uranus is the planet with the strongest affinity to eras, to that "Uranian eros" which is the basic force behind sociability and homophilia, but misunderstood and sometimes branded as neurotic homosexuality.

Chapter 2

THE NATURE OF
HOMOSEXUALITY

Concepts and explanations of homosexuality have always differed widely depending upon the point of view assumed. These were strongly influenced around 1865 by the erroneous ideas of K. H. Ulrichs as well as by homosexuality's at one time most prominent advocate, Dr. Magnus Hirschfeld. According to these two men homosexuality is attributable to a constitutional anomaly-a sexual "intermediate step." The work of Steinach seemed to contain more scientific confirmations, but any expectations that the problem would eventually be explained solely in terms of constitution have not been fulfilled; the physical bisexuality which can be shown to exist in every human being does not with all its gradations provide an explanation.

The fact that in every human there are physical traits of the opposite sex received particular emphasis in the works of W. Fliess, as did also the fact that among creative men there was beyond the usual mixture and without expense to their masculinity-an unusually greater emphasis of femininity. In reality, facts independent of each other have been taken to be causally related, and homosexuality is unexplainable from the physical side of the sexual constitution.

In contrast to this pathological interpretation of male homosexuality there exists the actual role which it plays in other aspects of social life, and this role is known as *eros*." (The word *eros* has been used with quite different meanings by other authors. Freud, for example, used it to connote the life instincts when these were being considered in a generally speculative way. Somewhat unaccountably, Heimsoth sometimes uses the word erotic to refer to his concept of eras and at other times with the usual connotations of the word. The reader should be alert to these shifts of meaning depending on context.) This male eros has not been analyzed in all its sociological, pedagogical, and philosophical connotations. Knowledge of its nature and positive value was correctly understood in ancient Greece, and one writer has shown by a collection of hundreds of quotations from classic German literature that this knowledge has by no means disappeared, while in more recent times the same concept was described before psychoanalysis by Benedict Friedlander, Gustav Jager, and Elisabeth von Kuppfer.

Unconcerned with this tradition, psychoanalysis had to find out for itself that in each man there are two sexual components present—the one towards the opposite and the other towards the same sex. The problem of homosexuality does not only present an important particular problem, but is a significant element in many other problems as, for example, in the organization of society and the leadership within it, and the propagation of knowledge; and therefore my conception, which has been formulated through my psychoanalytical practice, is neither that it is a perversity—which would imply it was acquired—nor a neurosis or perversion. Nor do I consider it the result of a strong manifestation—perhaps constitutionally conditioned—of one of the component instincts of Freud's sexual theory. My own concept is the same as that formulated by Dr. W. Stekel in his "Onanism and Homosexuality," volume 2 of his *Disturbances of the Instinctual and Emotional Life*.

Alongside of the drive which insures the reproduction of the

The Nature of Homosexuality

species and which is oriented to the opposite sex there exists a drive oriented towards the same sex which forms the basis of social cohesiveness extending beyond family and relations. Sociability, friendship, affection between friends, the male eros, camaraderie, homophilia, male societies, and pedagogy are phenomena that have some relationship to it.

Both components are present in every human being, and neither the one nor the other is ever wholly predominant, but instead one is always present at least in latency. It is evident in psychoanalysis in the transference process that this homosexual component is never absent, and this transference can also be cited as proof that the homosexual components are present in everyone and can be increased to the point of overt expression, when even among clearly exclusive heterosexuals they show an unmistakable sexual character. This becomes clear during the psychoanalysis of "normal" individuals by one of the same sex. I should emphasize that by an increased transference I do not refer solely to the result of a re-living of infantile fixations brought out during analysis, since in fact during manifestations of the homosexual components and the displacement of their object the transference reaction remains both qualitatively and quantitatively slight.

Both components can be easily diverted and therefore gratified indirectly. For example, the Don Juan pursues women without any complete satisfaction because he is really seeking another male. Other examples are a *tertium cohabitationis*, where two men are with one woman and therefore experience an indirect sexual contact, the bordello complex, and even jealousy; all appear to be conditioned by homosexual factors. The use of alcohol, and even more so cocaine and morphine, has a specific and particularly close relationship to homosexuality. Furthermore, there are men whose love lives are heterosexual but are primarily shaped by homosexual components, and psychoanalysis must at times label as "homosexual" certain individuals whose love life and conscious attitude appears to be completely heterosexual and who have never had anything to do with homosexual activities. Among the cases given later we will show some examples of these "masked" characteristics.

There also exist in every man two different kinds of possibilities of attraction. One is towards complement—towards one's polar opposite—and is heterophilic, as in heterosexuality and in sexuality or libido as distinct from eros; the other is directed towards the same sex, is homophilic, and is found all the way from the "homosexual" love between friends to the "heterosexual" companionate marriage; in other words, with always the widest possibilities of transformation and sublimation. Homophilia is more significantly bound up with eros than with sexuality.

Dr. Stekel's experience as a psychoanalyst resulted in the following formulation, which I quote here with some brief additional remarks.

All men are not only physically bisexual, but they also are bisexually oriented psychically. There are no exceptions to this rule. "Homosexual" and "heterosexual" can only be used for the two bisexuality components in the sense of tendency. The two components are qualitatively and quantitatively different in any individual and their relationship can only be determined by psychoanalysis. After the amphisexuality of the small child bisexuality manifests itself among normal men during puberty. The "heterosexual" then represses the greater part of his "homosexuality," but under influences which let down barriers, such as alcohol, cocain, or the process of transference in psychoanalysis, the remaining part of the "homosexual" components again becomes quite clear. A portion of the "homosexual" tendencies are sublimated into friendship, social activities, clubs and organizations, and nationalism. If this sublimation or repression miscarries he then becomes disposed to neurosis. Since every clearly heterosexual man cannot completely overpower his "homosexuality," he therefore carries the disposition to neurosis in himself. The stronger the repression the greater the possibility of a "negative" reaction which can even lead to paranoia (cf. Freud's theory of paranoia). But if the "heterosexuality" is repressed or sublimated then "homosexuality" arises. For the "homosexual" the heterosexuality which is not repressed or overcome also appears as a disposition to neurosis. The more certainly his heterosexuality is sublimated the more the homosexual is able to give the appearance of a normal male, and he then resembles the normal heterosexual.

For the normal "homosexual" this sublimation process appears more difficult than for the heterosexual and therefore these types are seen more seldom.

Analysis enables one to recognize the more frequent and typical defense reactions which Freud has shown to be anxiety, shame, disgust and hatred. The heterosexual feels disgust for homosexual acts and his reaction is indeed negative, but it has an affective content since disgust is only desire with negative affect. Frequently the homosexual has this aversion for women, which marks him as neurotic; or he hates women. The "normal" homosexual would have to be indifferent to women—and in fact it is so.

There is no one-sided "homosexuality" and there is no one-sided "heterosexuality," there is only bisexuality, and monosexuality is already a disposition to neurosis and in many cases a neurosis itself. These considerations result in the inescapable conclusion that the healthy man must be active bisexually.

In order to correct misunderstandings that erroneously identify the classical word *pederasty* with (the Latin) *pedicatio* we quote an observation of Freud: "The sexual role of the anal mucus membrane is in no way restricted to intercourse between men; its preference has no characteristics in common with inversion. It seems on the contrary that *pedicatio* of the male owes its role to the analogy with the act with women" (*Collected Works*, 5, 25). "Among men intercourse per anum does not at all concur with inversion" (*Collected Works* 5, 19). Hirschfeld's statistics, which are questionable, mention an occurrence of only eight percent of this kind of practice.

Freud indeed recognized both these components, but wrote in 1923 in "Neurotic Mechanisms in Jealousy, Paranoia, and Homosexuality" (*Collected Works*, 5):

> Attachment to the mother, narcissism, castration fear—we have heretofore found these in no way specific factors to be present in the psychic etiology of homosexuality, and to them must be added the influence of seduction, which causes the early fixation of the libido, as well as the influence of an organic factor which favors a passive role in the love life.

Although an ever-present bisexuality is recognized and admitted by every psychoanalyst, and some specific relationship of the two components is assumed where homosexuality has appeared, there has also been an attempt to attribute this to a specific erotogenic zone or a specific fixation of the libido in a pregenital stage. An example of this is P. Schilder's close identification of homosexuality with anal and sadistic tendencies.

I reject the explanation of homosexuality in terms of the constitutional factor as was described, for example, by Hirschfeld, because even among individuals whose sexual activity is exclusively homosexual, the factor of constitution does not always appear to explain it. And in view of my theory of the character-constellation described above I believe it is neither necessary nor possible to explain such activity as effects of the physical factors of bisexuality that are always present though in varying or different proportions. And finally I must reject any explanation based on the development of the libido through specific zone erogeneity; more will be said about this in chapters 6 and 10.

It is instead a matter of a bisexuality of mentality or character which appears in individuals in a different quantitative relationship.

These same factors play a role in masculine organizations, in love between friends, in the male eros, and the elements resulting from analysis of the individual are the same as those participating in the synthesis of society. The meaning of homosexuality is unmistakable; it is no "purposeless' perversion and not only occurs in nature but is demanded by nature. Its purposefulness must have an influence on the concept of the problem as a whole as well as its elucidation, but even more so on the concept of a therapeutic purpose. The question arises of the limits of the possibilities of psychotherapeutic influence, and this problem is frequently seen when the therapist desires to restore the patient to "normality." In such a case the "cure" might well be only some kind of heterosexual impotence. For the most part, the therapeutic goal ought instead to concentrate on the heterosexual component, since a complete suppression of the homosexual component would be neither possible nor desirable and, as Stekel showed, would lead to further neurotic behavior.

However, there remain always the individual peculiarities, the specific character-constellation of homosexuality, as I indicated in "The Psychoanalytic Concept of Homosexuality" which appeared in the *Rassegna di Studi Sessuali* in Rome:

> We cannot, even if we have mapped out all the psychic mechanisms involved, index all the individual particularities of homosexuality that will occur in any group of individuals. For example, cases occur with a quite striking preponderance of homosexual factors which, however, are quite without any apparent loss of heterosexuality, or there are cases of men with a male eros penetrating their entire nature and resulting in an

eros-type attractive power, but which is never sexualized, and where we can in no way find any indications of a mechanism of any repression. Others show a chronic failure and misfortune in their love life without any homosexual factors appearing to explain it. Or even some kind of traumaphilia of their heterosexuality. Or cases where some small but critical stimulus in the heterosexual life has been sufficient to lead the individual into homosexuality without this basic component seeming to receive any particular emphasis. Or cases where the two basic components seem about equal in strength and the question must remain open why the homosexuality so completely suppressed the heterosexuality. Or those cases where homosexuality apparently sets the stage for an unexplainable tendency to neurotic reactions, inhibitions, paranoid tendencies, and the use of drugs.

Of course it should always be emphasized that homosexuality—be it latent or manifest—as indeed all sexuality, can only be studied in connection with the totality of individual character and that it has roots going deep into each human character and is only a single factor in the character-constellation.

Homosexuality is clearly to be considered as having a closer relationship to schizothymia, or to the schizophrenia group. To go straight to an extreme example: The relationship of paranoia to-homosexuality has been completely elucidated, the relationships are considered proved and the knowledge of this relationship is certain. Etiologically paranoia is attributable to a strong repression of homosexuality (cf. Freud, Ferenczi, and especially Schilder). Stekel considered homosexuality, as well as every monosexual behavior, as a deviation from fundamental bisexual characteristics and activity and therefore already leading to the incipient stages of paralogia or psychosis. On the other hand A. Kronfeld, for example, is of the opinion that "perversions" require a basis of "paranoid traits." The relationships of schizophrenia to narcissism, which has many similarities to homosexuality, are clearly proved (again, cf. Schilder).

Not only in the psychiatric area, but also in the area of characterology, peculiarities in homosexuality are found which can take us further. Tragedy, or rather the tragic factor, is very strong in homosexuality. I have treated the theme already in a small work and came to the conclusion that this tragic factor has meaning and purpose and belongs to the essential nature of homosexuality. This tragic sense shows itself in the restlessness, in the lack of complete fulfillment through a melding of individuals, in the type of attraction and destiny involved, and lies in an "eternal departure of the beloved" in the words of Hans Bluher. I wrote in 1924: "The tragic situation of homosexuality lies in the nature of its ever binding and never releasing, in its ever-compelling eros. Here there is no feeling of fulfillment or complement—no release, only a temporary loosening, and so homosexuality is a tragic fate." (H. Bluher, A. Kronfeld, Alb. H. Rausch have described details concerning the problem.)

This basic feature we noted earlier to be typical for the schizothymics. Bleuler also emphasized the importance and the value of the schizoid element present in every man. While pure pyknic forms result only after reaching a certain age, *dementia praecox* belongs to this other group, and the physical structure at the time of adolescent growth is leptosomic. Puberty with its primarily schizothymic psychology and its strongly bisexual orientation again points to the creative individual (I am thinking of Goethe's observations on "repeated puberty."). Stekel considered homosexuality as a partially atavistic and regressive form, and it is true that certain archaic elements are unmistakable in its structure. So once again we see connections between masculinity in youth and schizothymia.

All these characteristics described indicate that homosexuality is connected with the schizothymic character and therefore confirm the observations made along these lines by Kretschmer.

It is necessary to conclude this section by establishing the links that connect homosexuality, paranoia, the schizothymic character, and the asthenic-athletic-dysplastic physical types. To this end the studies of A. Weil are significant. He discovered, for example, that among homosexuals the relationship of the measurement from the tip of the coccyx to the horizontal plane formed by the parietal bones tends to be less than the measurement from the coccyx to the base. Weil also established that both Kretschmer's "dysplastic" group and the more extreme asthenic types showed an above-average tendency to homosexual activity. In one group of about 300 homosexuals Weil found the asthenic type to account for 70 percent; according to a work published in 1924 he found in a group of 370 homosexuals only three pyknics, a third to be asthenoeunuchoid, a third asthenic, and the remaining third to show feminine sexual characteristics. The percentage of dysplastics is therefore divided here as well between the tall, infantile-appearing types and those individuals showing marked traits of the opposite sex. I have mentioned that this is apparently the basis for the actually inaccurate stereotype of the homosexual as a very tall, thin, "degenere superieur." In any case the complete absurdity of the hypothesis of M. Hirschfeld concerning his "intermediate steps" can be seen. It is pretty clearly shown that the physical type of predominantly homosexual individuals does not incline to be either asexual or demonstrating characteristics of the opposite sex.

Finally then, it appears that there exists a strong connection between the asthenic type and a generally schizothymic character, while cases of "intersexual" types are less significant for the entire question of male homosexuality. The pyknic types—that is, the earth and water signs of astrology—appear not to be particularly disposed. While there exists an area of partial similarity to physical types that incline to show female characteristics, the far greater tendency is to the extreme asthenic-athletic types and schizothymic character. These latter traits, as stated in the last chapter, are typically and characteristically masculine.

Chapter 3

CHARACTER-
CONSTELLATION

Constitution is the individual physical nature given at birth;
the influence of environment and milieu then work on this.
Development is begun and various reactions are set in motion,
and this ever-developing organism is then referred to as the condition by Tandler and J. Bauer, for example, as well as others.
For them the condition is the specific individual state at any
given moment, and is based upon the physical *constitution*. The
concept of constitution was changed by Kretschmer and used as
a designation of physique types, and it was only in this sense that
one could then speak of "like" or "similar" constitutions. These
constitutional types were then correlated with certain psychological types.

However, I am of the opinion that along with these concepts
there is also a specific characterological type which is not at all
so closely connected with the physical constitution or the condition as has been commonly supposed. I shall show that practi-
cally identical constitutions do not necessarily demonstrate like
character, and for this purpose I want to consider the cases of the
two monozygotic male twins A. and K. H.

This factor, which is independent of the physical constitution and yet which characterizes the predispositions of the personality, I call the constellation. As stated, I have good reasons for using twins in introducing my concept of the constellation. The problem of twins has been considered up to now from only biological or physiological points of view. But what would the scientific community have to say about such a case as the following that was described in an article in a Vienna newspaper in the middle of November 1927?

> Twin sisters become mothers at the same time. . . .
> Twin sisters, who live three thousand miles from each other, have become mothers of two children on the same day and at the same hour, according to London newspaper reports. The women were a Mrs. J. Bartram, who under her maiden-name Juliette Hall Crompton was well-known in America as a stage and film star, and who now lives in London, and a Mrs. M. Coblentz from Baltimore. The two twin sisters were from earliest childhood closely connected by inner bonds and these seem to have repeated themselves later through a series of remarkable coincidental occurrences. Thus two years ago Mrs. Bartram had a nervous breakdown and at the same time her sister also became seriously ill. It is interesting that both sisters entered into a secret marriage at the same time and were married on the same day.

It is astrology, however, that would allow one to perceive the necessary dependence of actual life events, but this is a problem that has not received the notice that it deserves. I remember, for example, a case mentioned to me by the astrologer Sindbad which concerned two twins born in 1876 and where one committed suicide by drowning in May 1922, while the other came to the same fate in August 1922.

And I recollect cases from the World War where twins were injured in the same part of the body on the field at about the same time. For example, in one case one received a strafe wound on the shin and the twin brother, whom I knew personally, received a wound in the calf from an exploding grenade eleven days later. When he received news about his brother who had been wounded eleven days earlier he joked: "It's always been like that! My brother once fell from his horse and hurt his hand badly, and ten days later I gave him a little competition by falling off my bicycle with exactly the same result!"

However, in such cases not only similarities are found, but despite the same constitution extensive differences of character can also be found, and these are the differences of *constellation* whose independence from the physical constitution can be clearly proved and whose differences can be determined by astrological means.

My interest in the problem of similar events occurring at nearly the same time in the lives of twins—even events resulting from factors that would usually be considered exogenous—was the reason for getting to know the twin brothers A. and K. H., who were born in the last days of 1907. Both are practicing dentists. The similarity in appearance is extremely striking-both are large and well-proportioned, appearing to be about twenty-four or twenty-five years old, and have a combined athletic and asthenic physique, well-proportioned Anglo-Saxon profile, gray-blue eyes and thick, wavy blond hair. Neither can be distinguished from the other, except for one small birthmark located in different places. The first-born, A.H., has his above the left cheekbone in the area where the beard and hair of the head come together; the "younger" K. H. has a more oval-shaped one on the edge of the lower left jaw. The resemblance is really unusual; on the above left side both have a *dens caninus* which has not changed in twenty years, and both have had chronic catarrh of the frontal sinus since March 1922.

These are, of course, monozygotic twins. Twin pregnancies are in about eighty-five percent of cases dizygotic, monozygotic only in fifteen percent of cases. Monozygotic twins are not only of the same sex but have a similarity of constitution which is so extensive that for practical purposes their constitutions may be considered to be identical.

Both these twins have the same general points of view and outlook and are the products of the same environment, and both have almost always been together. And yet their characters are really quite different! I should mention that I had known the two men only by sight and therefore had no idea of the differences in their characters. I was interested in hearing about any similarity of external events in their lives whose nature would be demonstrable by astrology, and I mentioned this interest to them in a very general way. They had themselves been struck by such similarities and had been unable to find an explanation they could accept. At my request they gave in their own words what were the differences between their characters, which is what I give here, less details.

The "older" A. H. was more easily excitable and somewhat more inclined to anger, while the "younger" K. H. was more reticent and was less inclined to seek out contact with people, though he had a more engaging personality. I learned that the "older" twin was more interested in practical aspects of technology, while his brother was more inclined to his studies and other side interests. In the following examination of the horoscopes these differences are easy to see. In any case, the same constitution has resulted in significantly different characters, or to use our term—different *constellations*! And the basis for this difference of character is that there was a lapse of more than two hours between their birth times!

Figures 1 and 2 are the two horoscopes, where the difference between the change of the eastern meridian due to the rotation of the earth during that interval and the resulting difference in the house position of the planets can be seen, though their own proper motion is minimal.

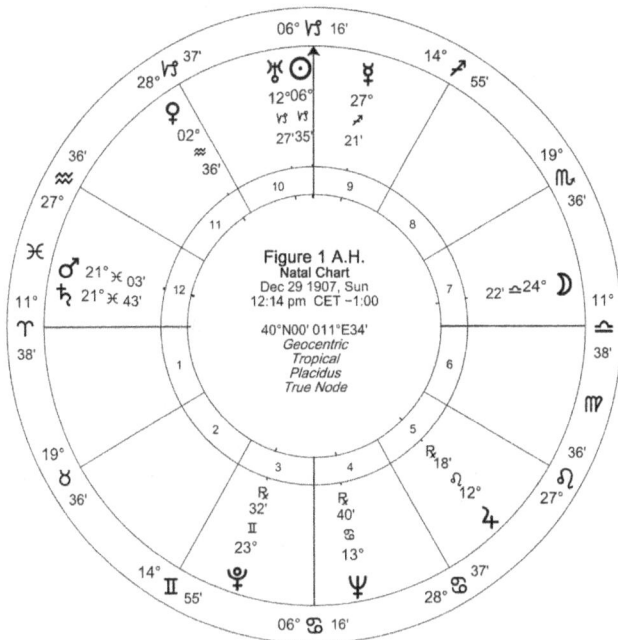

Figure 1 A.H.
Natal Chart
Dec 29 1907, Sun
12:14 pm CET −1:00
40°N00' 011°E34'
Geocentric
Tropical
Placidus
True Node

From the horoscope it is clear that the "older" A.H. is the more energetic and active, as his horoscope ruler is Mars, and his Ascendant is in the first decanate of Aries. He dislikes making compromises and easily breaks down opposition; his interests are primarily concerned with his profession (Sun in tenth square Ascendant) and in this career he will remain at the top (Sun conjunction Midheaven), but he is restless in his profession, and there is a tendency to instability and change (Uranus in the tenth square Ascendant, Uranus parallel Sun), brought on partly by disturbing factors inherited or caused by the father (retrograde Neptune in the fourth square Ascendant opposition Uranus, Pisces in the twelfth!). A certain nervousness affects the inclination to refined friendships with women (Venus in Aquarius in the eleventh, Venus parallel retrograde Neptune). There have been many strongly emotional relationships with women, but subject to frequent changes (Moon in seventh, Cancer on the

Homosexuality in the Horoscope   41

cusp of the fifth); a mother identification (Cancer on the cusp of the fourth). He is successful in his love life, but also has serious inhibitions (retrograde Jupiter moving toward the cusp of the sixth house, and ruler of the ninth and the sign intercepted in the twelfth house, Jupiter sesquisquare Mercury in the ninth is mitigated by Jupiter trine Ascendant; Moon sextile Mercury, Moon parallel Mars), chiefly on account of a repressed and possibly inherited sadistic streak (Mars conjunction Saturn in the twelfth house in an intercepted sign) that will work out also in irritability and moodiness, secret enmity and isolation.

The "younger" K. H., on the other hand, appears to us to be an intellectual person interested in theories, while less impulsive and practical (Mercury is ruler of the horoscope). Just because of his shy reticence and his popularity he will do well in his profession (Venus conjunction Midheaven, trine Ascendant). He is more interested in metaphysics than in his profession (Sun moving to the cusp of the ninth house) and has a less striking personality (horoscope ruler is in exile at the cusp of the eighth house; its dispositor retrograde Jupiter in the fourth house), but he has a very free and even eccentric philosophy of life (Uranus conjunction Sun, Uranus at the cusp of the ninth). He is not very practical (retrograde Neptune at the cusp of the third), is to some extent irritated by his brother (Neptune in the third house), has considerable nervousness (Moon in the sixth), is incapable of coming out of himself, and there are extensive inhibitions in the area of friendships (Mars conjunction Saturn in a sign intercepted in the eleventh house) so that at times this will be an area of disputes and losses.

After knowing that Aries rises in the horoscope of A. H. one notices, in comparison with K. H., a lighter temple formation. There is also another small but significant constitutional difference: The Mars brother, A. H., has the same physical size but is from 1.5 to 3 kilos heavier, while his chest and pelvic measurements are larger than those of his Mercury brother. I recall my earlier statement that the Aries type is athletic-asthenic, while

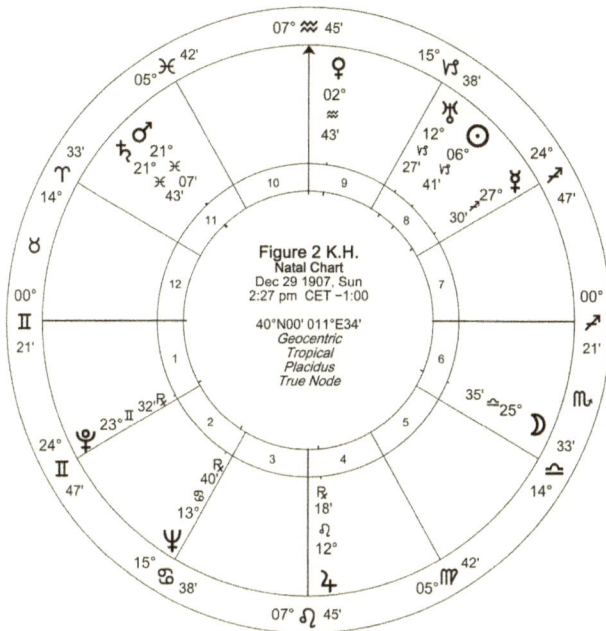

Figure 2 K.H.
Natal Chart
Dec 29 1907, Sun
2:27 pm CET –1:00

40°N00' 011°E34'
Geocentric
Tropical
Placidus
True Node

the Gemini type is considered asthenic. The influence of the difference in the Ascendants is remarkable, and it must be stated as well that the identity of constitution, which is assumed to be inescapable from its monozygotic origin, cannot explain it. A study of heredity in connection with astrology might further explain the problem. In any case, the two horoscope rulers—Mars for the first-born and Mercury for the last-born—are seen to be further connected through a square, and I feel this connection is specifically related to their heredity. Thus, another brother of the twins has Ascendant Aries 15°44' and Mars at 25°43' Leo conjunction Venus at 25°24' Leo near the cusp of the sixth house at 28° Leo; he also has Pisces intercepted in the twelfth with retrograde Saturn at 11°35' Pisces.

Naturally, the similarities of character are important: The rampant individuality (Sun in Capricorn), albeit proceeding in different directions, the relatively balanced emotional life (Moon

Homosexuality in the Horoscope   43

in Libra), the almost too broad range of intellect with a somewhat exaggerated sense of justice (Mercury in exile, its dispositor Jupiter in the second decanate of Leo), the more intellectual feeling for women rather than crassly sexual (Venus in Aquarius). On the other hand there is the persistent and even vengefully aggressive will, which is at the same time held in check (Mars and Saturn conjunct in the intercepted sign Pisces). This conjunction was significant for A. H. in that when the Ascendant had progressed to the semi-square of Mars the chronic catarrh of the frontal sinus began, while with K. H. the onset of the same condition was shown by the Ascendant progressed to the square of Mars.

The two sets of character traits were completely established to my satisfaction, and the psychological side of the problem is therefore clarified here by astrology, and the character difference—the difference in the constellations of the twins whose constitutions were identical—rests in the final analysis upon the difference of the two hours in their births.

I believe that I have shown with this case of the twins A. and K. H. that not only a different character-constellation can occur where the constitution is identical, but that it can be ascertained as well.

In considering the constellation I take into account only the radix or birth horoscope and deliberately leave the directions out. I use the concept of the constellation in the study of character in a way similar to the condition concept, which rests in turn upon the constitution and its given physical structure. On the latter the course of life under all circumstances is built. And with respect to this we should keep in mind the well-known aphorism in astrology: No directions can bring about what is not already shown in the radix horoscope. Directions can only produce development, they cannot signify something entirely new.

Chapter 4

PSYCHOANALYSIS

The character-constellation has up to now been neither comprehended nor measured because of its relative independence
from the physical constitution and the condition. However, it
can be correctly understood or realized by means of astrology.

The problem is not without significance in practice, and this
is shown by the following case described to me by a colleague.
It was another case of twins, but it was many years ago and,
unfortunately, at that time I did not have sufficient technical
knowledge of astrology and its practical value and therefore did
not trouble myself to obtain the horoscope data. In any case, one
of these twins underwent analysis in order to free himself of his
homosexuality; the other twin was heterosexual and without any
neurotic peculiarities.

The analysis proceeded very well according to the analyst,
who was of the opinion that the patient's homosexuality was
"only psychogenic," that is, neurotically conditioned and therefore "curable," since a conditioning based on the constitution
could be excluded, as his identical twin was heterosexual. If I
remember correctly, this case has even been cited in the literature
as an argument against the "inborn nature of homosexuality."
The analyst found the following mechanisms: narcissism pro-

jected on the brother; a strong rejection of the mother because of her preference for the brother, as well as a strong identification on the part of the patient for his brother, and then finally an overwhelming sexual differentiation from both the mother and the brother; the father played no significant role.

The result of this long and involved analysis was nil: Incidental neurotic symptoms related to social and professional pressures disappeared, but the homosexuality "in no ways conditioned by constitution" remained as a positive fact and there were no heterosexual inclinations. Of course, I am of the opinion that for these twins the character-constellation—in the sense that this has been formulated—played the decisive role. In any case, the understanding furnished by astrology is reliable and useful in practice, as I hope to show in giving an interpretation through both astrology and analytical methods of a case from my own practice.

The case was that of the twenty-two year old Scandinavian, F. H., who came to me on account of his impotence and to have it removed by psychotherapy. However, as he had only a twelve-day stay in town before returning to his homeland, I decided to use every means possible to arrive at a swift diagnosis.

In his horoscope two features struck the eye immediately: The horoscope ruler, the Sun, as well as Uranus, were both in the fifth house of love and children and intercepted in the sign Sagittarius, while Venus was in the sixth house of illness.

On the cusp of the sixth house was Capricorn, whose ruler Saturn was in domicile at 16°11' Aquarius and therefore in opposition to the Ascendant. Saturn's important influence is further shown by its sextile to the Sun intercepted in the fifth house and its semi-square to Venus in the sixth.

Venus in the sixth house of illness gives further indications. It is peregrine in an earth sign, and as ruler of the eleventh house describes a nature more eros-inclined than sexual in its relationships with the opposite sex. The planet has reference to the

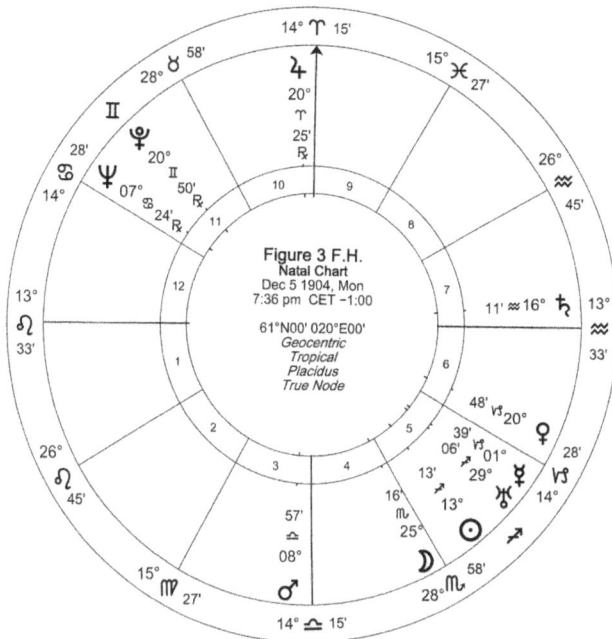

Figure 3 F.H.
Natal Chart
Dec 5 1904, Mon
7:36 pm CET −1:00

61°N00' 020°E00'
Geocentric
Tropical
Placidus
True Node

fourth house, which has Libra is on that cusp. Near this cusp is Mars at 8°57' Libra, showing some connection with younger male siblings. In the fourth house, but drawing near to the cusp of the fifth, is the Moon that, because of this house position, has reference to the mother; the Moon is in exile in Scorpio. Venus has a sextile from the Moon, but will not receive a favorable influence from this Moon since not only is it in fall but also is in relationship to the house of secret weaknesses as Cancer lies on the cusp of the twelfth. From the standpoint of psychoanalysis we must assume as a result of the Moon sextile Venus that there is a mother fixation with an unfavorable result. The fact that the Moon is in Scorpio and in the fourth house gives to the Mars signs in this horoscope yet another connection with the native 's family.

Before we pass on to the aspects of Venus (in the sixth and square retrograde Jupiter, parallel Uranus as well as sextile the

Homosexuality in the Horoscope   47

Moon), let us examine his sexuality as seen from the fifth house. Since the cusp of this house is in 28°58' Scorpio, and Mars is the ruler, we come once again to Mars—symbol of a younger brother, as it is located in the third house. The other Mars sign, Aries, is on the Midheaven at 14°, and in the tenth house retrograde. The aspects of Mars do not take us much further, although its sextile to the Sun, the horoscope ruler and located in the fifth house, shows the great significance the brother has for the native's love life, while Mars square retrograde Neptune in the eleventh, but drawing close to the cusp of the twelfth house, gives some cause for concern.

But the greatest significance for the sexuality of the individual lies in the fact that there are three planets in the fifth house, and two of these are intercepted in the sign Sagittarius. Intercepted signs, as well as retrograde planets, must be considered from the point of view of psychoanalysis as standing for repressed neurotic elements related to their house or sign positions, etc. The ruler of this intercepted Sagittarius is Jupiter, which is strong in its own decanate of Aries but is also retrograde at the cusp of the tenth house. Because of its position in a Mars sign (the family!) we must realize that this Jupiter has some connection with the father and, on account of its retrograde motion, will work in some strongly inhibiting way. Along with this we can assign some similar effect to the philosophical outlook of the native, since the cusp of the ninth is located at 15° Pisces, and Jupiter is therefore the ruler of this house as well. The influence of Jupiter through its retrograde motion alone could be seen as a neurotic mechanism, which becomes more specific by Jupiter sending an exact square to Venus in the sixth. The so-called "castration complex" can be assumed as clearly shown. But from the sign Aries where Jupiter is located we have a third indication that there are difficulties indirectly connected with the Mars brother.

Unfortunately, the otherwise favorable individuality (Sun trine Ascendant) suffers from a neurotic inhibition, because the Sun at 13°13' Sagittarius is located in the fifth house in an intercepted sign. Taken in all, its aspects are of a dubious character: In addition to the sextile already mentioned of Mars from the third house, through which the specific importance of Mars is shown, there is also a sextile from Saturn, which is ruler of the house of illness and furthermore standing in opposition to the Ascendant. There is also a close parallel to Neptune retrograde in the house of friendships, but drawing close to the cusp of the twelfth house; this means danger from something more than neurosis—that is, narcotics.

However, even more meaningful for the sexual orientation is Uranus—also located in the fifth house and intercepted in Sagittarius; Uranus is also conjunct Mercury at 1°39' Capricorn. Generally speaking, Uranus is the most striking significator and representative of the homosexual factor. But not all those who have Uranus in the house of love (the fifth) or of friendship (the eleventh) or of partnerships (the seventh) or of the self (the first) can be homosexual; otherwise a third of the population would be so. As Uranus in this case is intercepted in the fifth house of love, some repression along these lines is to be expected. The planet has two aspects: The first is a parallel to Venus in the sixth, which already is sufficient to show that a certain "illness" exists in sexual relationships with women—repressed homosexuality. But the second aspect is a conjunction with Mercury and is even more important in revealing the nature and origin of this neurotic and (apparently) latent homosexuality; Mercury rules Virgo and this sign is located on the cusp of the third. Therefore, we have a fourth connection with the brother!

Let us examine now the other Mercury sign, Gemini. This sign is intercepted in the eleventh house of friendships, so his attitude toward friendships is also neurotically conditioned, and in fact some disturbance in this area was quite evident. The cusp of the eleventh house is located at 28°58' Taurus, and the ruler Venus is posited in the sixth. In the eleventh house, however, there is another very interesting feature—the retrograde Neptune, which is drawing close to the cusp of the house of secret weaknesses and is ruler of the ninth house (a house significant for neurosis) since Pisces falls on the cusp of the ninth. But Neptune provides the fifth connection with the brother as it has, as we have already mentioned, a square to Mars.

Uranus also has a relationship to the seventh and eighth houses, as Aquarius is located on the cusp of these houses. The native could be a good friend, but partnerships are spoiled by the cold and powerful Saturn which is located in the seventh in wide opposition to the Ascendant and is ruler of the sixth house of illness.

This very significant Saturn sends an exact semi-square to Mercury in Capricorn, and Capricorn is on the cusp of the house of illness. This aspect provides a most significant link. Sun sextile Saturn underscores—since the Sun is the horoscope ruler—the importance of this Saturn, while Saturn's semi-sextile to Venus shows the direction in which his influence will operate, but the exact semisquare to Mercury pinpoints the problem; Mercury points to homosexuality (Mercury conjunction Uranus) and the younger brother.

Along with the psychological effects of the Moon (feelings) in fall and the stern and isolating Saturn in opposition to the ascendant, there is another indication which relates to physical factors that should not go unnoticed—the fact that the Moon is only 18 degrees behind the Sun. This is never a sign of a particularly strong sexual vitality.

We can now formulate the astrological material as follows: A neurotic mother fixation, strong inhibitions because of the father (the so-called "castration complex"), a negation of the whole sexuality resulting from repression, a homosexual factor connected with his younger brothers which has also disturbed his attitude toward, and his choice of, friends, and a tendency to the use of narcotics. The principal cause is a repressed homosexuality which remains latent but first arose through some connection with a brother.

During the analysis the following material was brought to light and is worth mentioning.

The patient's *first* dream after the beginning of the analysis, whose importance was emphasized by W. Stekel, was as follows: "I am in a theatre. On stage is some kind of variety act. Two clowns appear. What happens is hard to remember, and I cannot exactly say. After leaving the theatre I run into some girls, which surprises me." The analytical situation has been well-expressed in this dream; we find that the symbol of a theatre, where the complexes make their appearance and the patient sits watching, is frequent during analysis. The prognosis is favorable in that after leaving the theatre he "runs into" some girls, but his attitude towards analysis is skeptical since the concluding event of the dream surprises him, and he does not therefore anticipate much success. But I can add still more to the dream and its significance: The patient is, as was said, a Scandinavian, and we had a certain difficulty because of knowing each other's language imperfectly, but the clowns were apparently a male and a female, and their clothing was white and resembled nightshirts. There was some playing around that had a sexual overtone. This material reminds us immediately of the playing around that children do while getting in or going to bed; the patient is the oldest of four brothers.

But there is nothing here of games of an otherwise homosexual nature. That they are not remembered as such is no proof that they are not, however, and it would even be surprising if the repressed material had come to light so soon.

When the patient was ten years old he heard his father say to his mother that he hated him but liked the other brothers, and this was frightening to the child. The marriage of the parents was a good one, and the patient mentioned this at the first interview, though the father was tyrannical, and the only child the father appeared to dislike was the patient. And finally, a significant factor seems to be that the next oldest brother, who was 3.75 years younger than the patient, turned out to be very much like the father.

I have already mentioned that the parents' marriage was a happy one. The patient recalled a dream that took place years before: "A woman completely unknown to me comes rushing into my room. She is very beautiful and has a small child in her arm. She is running away from her husband and wants to hide with me. She trusts me completely. Later she lays the child down in the corner and after that she gets into bed with me and there is some sexual activity." The patient became enthusiastic: "That this strange wild woman had so much trust in me. That was really beautiful!"

The antithetical point is that a woman whom he knows very well has no such trust in him: his *mother*! I explained the dream to him, and the patient at first rejected it, but in a few days he came back on his own to this dream and confessed that this woman whom he had "never seen before or after" was an idealized version of his mother. We now see the mother fixation which had been indicated in the horoscope.

The patient went through a period of heavy drinking, even despite the Prohibition in Norway. Also, a period of using cocaine came and went without the homosexual tendencies coming to the surface. But according to analysis and experience this is an indication of the neurotic damage already done and the earlier repression of his homosexual tendencies.

His fiancee is the currently fashionable boyish type.

In the past the patient had two accidents. On one occasion he fell from a horse which then stepped on him, and this occurred on the birthday of the next younger brother. The brother also rode this horse. And the year before, also on the birthday of the brother, he had an accident and hurt his ring finger badly, as well as the rest of his hand, and in fact the scar prevents him from wearing any engagement ring!

I began therapy, which included two periods of hypnosis. I also asked for the birthdate of the brother. At the time of the birth the patient was not yet four years old but he recalls being awakened in the early morning hours by the commotion at the arrival of his little brother; nevertheless, the exact time is not known.

The following astrological material will be striking to anyone familiar with what has been said already.

Venus, which is in 20° Capricorn and in the sixth house of the patient's horoscope, is conjunct the brother's Uranus retrograde at 17° Capricorn, and retrograde Jupiter at 20° Aries in the patient's horoscope, which is significant for his Venus because of the square between these two planets, is conjunct the brother's Saturn retrograde at 22° Aries. Though the birthtime is not known exactly, there exists a range of possibilities extending from 7° Leo to the last degrees of Leo for the brother's Ascendant. But I know from my astrological research with respect to heredity that it can be assumed that the brother's Ascendant is in all probability very close to that of the patient. In such a case the brother's retrograde Uranus would be right on the cusp of his own sixth house of illness where it would receive a close opposition of Neptune at 18° Cancer, and at the cusp of the twelfth of secret enemies. The character of the brother makes these deductions for him seem admissible, judging from certain details I was able to get from what the patient said about him. In any case, the brother was the more sickly. The patient knows nothing at all about the brother's sexual orientation. A measurement was taken of the relationship between the coccyx and the crown and the coccyx and the base, and the former measurement was greater by 2cm, which bespeaks against a "constitutional" homosexuality (according to Weil).

Understandably, the analysis could not come to a satisfactory conclusion in only twelve daily sessions. But the various fragments made possible at least some understanding of the psychic mechanisms of F. H. I deliberately do not introduce here any directions or attempts to consider the case further with the aid of them, and for the brother there were no dates or starting points for any rectification of his horoscope. If there were it would in all probability be then possible to calculate the exact time of the trauma. For the rectification of the horoscope of F. H. the dates of the accident and the period of the use of drugs were used (for the latter: Ascendant progressed to sextile Neptune). This rectification resulted in the Ascendant being moved only about twenty minutes.

To get an opinion on a prognosis for the case, I consulted with my friend and teacher Captain F. Schwickert who, under the pen name Sindbad, has gained the greatest reputation for ability in these matters. He stated—and the reader can follow the calculations by himself—that during the time of treatment the Ascendant had progressed past the square to the Moon (25° Leo) and a more favorable period could now be expected. The period during 1929 and 1930 when the progressed Ascendant will trine Uranus need not be considered as a time of continuing difficulties, and the same is true for the period immediately following that when the Ascendant will trine Mercury. There is then no reason for worry during the next few years.

I had not had any word from F. H. as I was writing the case up for publication. But then suddenly after two months he reported a good improvement. "My nerves are better; I'm no longer so nervous and look forward to the future." The functional factor appears not to be completely adequate, but considering it was the work of only twelve days such a result could hardly be expected through psychoanalytic means alone.

In any case, it can be seen that the concept of the character-constellation is such that, as in this case, a psychoanalysis based even primarily on astrology is in certain cases quite possible.

Chapter 5

HOMOSEXUALITY AS CONSTELLATION

I introduced the case of A. and K. H. to show that in spite of the constitutional identity there exists a difference in character—a different *constellation*, whose nature can be determined by astrology, and I introduced F. H. to show the significance of this constellation for psychoanalytic practice. In the interpretation of the case of F. H. the specific situation concerning the brother was emphasized and also the general significance of planets in the fifth house, and in particular the planet Uranus.

Throughout this work, which considers in particular the characteristics of the individual sexuality and its corresponding constellation, attention should always be given first to the fifth house, which rules the love life, the sexuality, pleasures, and progeny—not only in the physical sense, but in the sense of creative works as well. But just as the seventh house is important in any consideration of the first—because of the reciprocal influence the houses lying opposite each other have—so the eleventh house is also of great interest as this house relates also to the subject of homosexuality.

Here some mention must be made of the important but seldom-discussed point, which Morinus established, that a given house represents an essential factor while the house lying opposite can supply indications for particular events. Sindbad paraphrases Morinus and says:

> Each house participates in the accidental meanings of the house lying opposite to it. But these accidental meanings of the opposite houses do not extend to their rulers, and the ruler cannot be used to assist in interpreting these meanings. A planet which is strong by its cosmic state contains much meaning for the house lying opposite, and one which is in a weak cosmic state has a correspondingly weaker meaning. But the opposition always points to a certain obstruction or antagonism in the realization of the affairs of the opposite house, while increasing the evil that may be indicated by this house.

Of course, in examining the fifth and eleventh houses it is not sufficient solely to consider the planets that are actually located in those houses, but other determining factors must be considered as well. The following points should therefore always be kept in mind:

1. The planet ruling the sign in which the particular house cusp falls.

2. The cosmic state of this planet—whether or not it has a dispositor, and the house location of both planets.

3. Possible aspects between the planet and others located in signs under its rulership.

4. The cosmic state of the planet actually present in the house under study—that is, a consideration of its dispositors.

5. The houses over which they rule.

6. The kind of aspects the planet actually located in the house has, from which planets in what kind of cosmic state, the locations of these latter and their own determinations.

7. Planets located in the opposite house and their cosmic state, their meanings and determinations.

8. Aspects to the cusp of the house in question.

Of course, it has not been possible to examine each of these details in the thirty horoscopes that follow; I underscore only what is characteristic for the sexual constellation. All the factors, for example, that could be deduced alone from the Ascendant are not given in the analysis. So, to begin, I will give a series of horoscopes in which, as in the case of F. H., Uranus is in the fifth house. This will illustrate how varying the circumstances can be that accompany a single recurring factor, and the frequently completely different dynamics to be found. In fact, Uranus in the fifth house will always indicate some more or less increased homosexuality (perhaps also in the sense of affecting the relationships with friends through the accidental factor of the opposite house as described above), but other elements in the individual's personality are always exerting an influence. I would say that for the manifestation of a homosexuality which is not simply occasional, several factors must always be involved. An analysis by astrology which is not strongly individual, but schematic and relying on ready-made phrases, will produce an unbelievable amount of nonsense (such as Uranus in the fifth, or bad aspects of Venus with Uranus, Saturn or Mars "cause homosexuality and perversions").

Figure 4

In the foreground of Figure 4, Frederick the Great, we see the strong individuality through the Sun trine ascendant, and this planet is also of great importance for the life's destiny since it is conjunct the Midheaven; Mars located further on in the tenth house is an indication of the same and points to the career as general (despite the opposition of the Moon and Saturn, the latter in exile and in turn disposed of by the Sun). The horoscope ruler Mercury is located in the tenth house but at the cusp of the

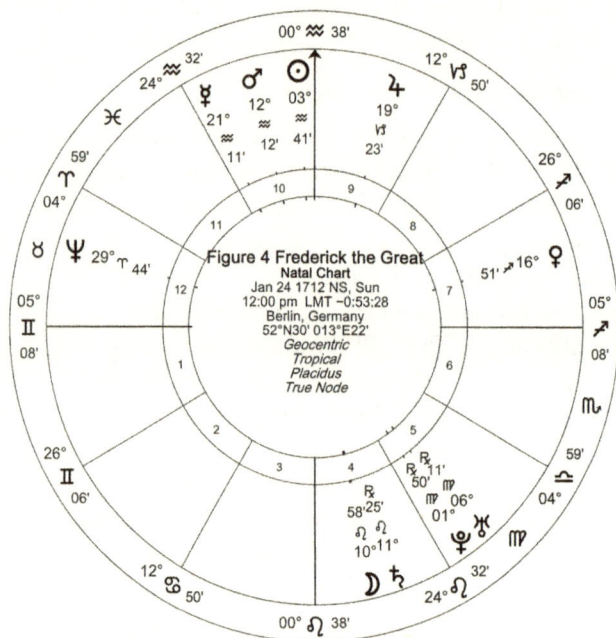

Figure 4 Frederick the Great
Natal Chart
Jan 24 1712 NS, Sun
12:00 pm LMT –0:53:28
Berlin, Germany
52°N30' 013°E22'
Geocentric
Tropical
Placidus
True Node

eleventh, showing his leadership, his influence, and the love he personally inspired through his humanity.

The Sun is ruler of the fifth house of love. Its position at the cusp of the tenth shows the capacity for sublimating his sexuality into his external life and career, but in the fifth house we also find the other Mercurial sign, Virgo, intercepted and containing Uranus. This Uranus sends a second aspect to the Ascendant— a close square—and thereby gains in importance, particularly since Uranus's sign, Aquarius, lies on the cusp of the tenth and the eleventh house of friendships. Uranus is rendered somewhat unfavorable by the fact that it receives a sextile from Neptune. Uranus in the fifth in an intercepted sign shows a homosexual complex that is neurotic and the Neptune aspect emphasizes this further since it is located in the sixth house of illness and is in turn intercepted in the Mars sign Scorpio. Perhaps this may also indicate a venereal infection since Neptune has a square to the

Sun, ruler of the fifth, and is the Sun's worst and closest aspect, and is moreover in a relationship to the eleventh house through the interception there of the sign Pisces.

Venus is not very favorable as it is ruler of the sixth house and of the sign intercepted in the twelfth, as well as located in the seventh house, which according to Morinus refers not only to unions but also to open enemies. Its sextile to Mercury and Mars results—through their rulerships, not their location—in the fact that he saw his gentleness as "feminine" and felt it was something to be rejected. Also, the rather wide trines to Venus from Jupiter, Moon, and Saturn in Leo in the fourth house are significant for his attitude to women. As ruler of Cancer in which the third house cusp falls, the Moon gives an important indication of his fixation on his sisters.

The horoscope ruler is located at the cusp of the eleventh house of friendships, and the co-ruler of the sign on this cusp—Saturn—is conjunct the Moon. Saturn is in exile and is disposed of by the Sun at the Midheaven with its capacity for sublimation already mentioned. Also, the Sun shows that his position was inherited as Leo is on the cusp of the fourth.

Along with the fifth house Uranus, it seems significant in this case that the horoscope ruler is located on the cusp of the eleventh house and in opposition to the cusp of the fifth, although both location and rulership indicate that homosexual and heterosexual components have been sublimated. Overt manifestation will be made difficult by the intercepted Uranus as well as by the intercepted sign in the eleventh house, which is ruled by Neptune in the sixth—a planet holding important aspects. Moreover, except for Uranus and Neptune all the planets are in masculine signs.

Figure 5

Figure 5 is the chart of Haarman, a man who during 1923 and 1924 murdered twenty-seven young people, mainly boys

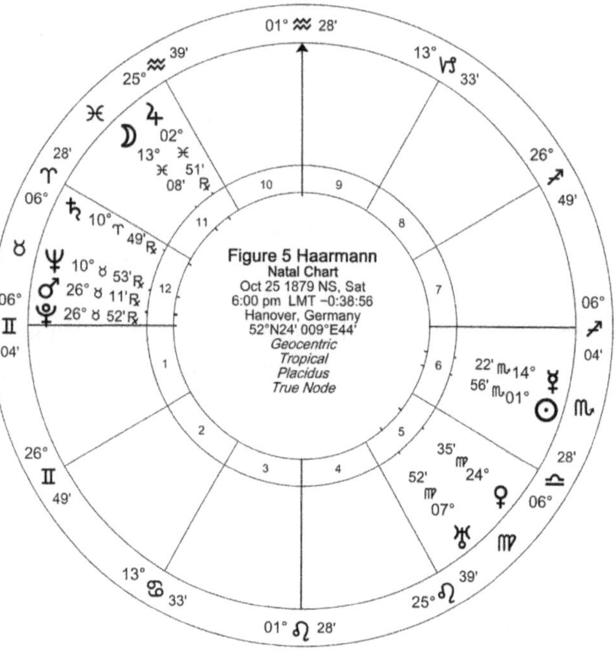

Figure 5 Haarmann
Natal Chart
Oct 25 1879 NS, Sat
6:00 pm LMT −0:38:56
Hanover, Germany
52°N24' 009°E44'
Geocentric
Tropical
Placidus
True Node

around eighteen years old, and hid the bodies. He had already been in prisons and asylums before this period of mass-murders began. After a sensational trial he was executed April 15, 1925. The case is said to have been the inspiration for Fritz Lang's classic movie of psychopathic horror, *M.* See C. E. O. Carter's *Some Principles of Horoscopic Delineation* for his analysis of the horoscope.

The first glance at Figure 5 immediately reveals how unusual this horoscope is. All planets are in intercepted signs except retrograde Saturn located just at the cusp of the twelfth house of secret enmity. Beyond that, all the planets above the horizon, with the exception of the Moon, are retrograde. The preponderance of feminine signs in the distribution of the planets is striking. As for the cosmic states of the planets—Jupiter is in domicile, Mars in exile, and Mars's dispositor Venus, as well as Saturn, are in the fifth, sixth, eleventh, and twelfth houses.

In the fifth house of sexuality we find Venus and Uranus intercepted in Virgo. Both assume special importance by the fact that the ruler of this intercepted sign, Mercury, is the ruler of the horoscope. The ruler of the fifth house is the Sun, which is in the sixth house of illness and intercepted in the sign Scorpio; it destroys his position (square the Midheaven!). The whole man is sick: Mercury, ruler of the horoscope, is likewise intercepted in the house of illness, and has in addition a destructive opposition from the retrograde Jupiter intercepted in the eleventh house.

The Ascendant receives two aspects. Saturn retrograde in an unfortunate house, but nonetheless the only planet which is not intercepted, sends a sextile, while Uranus intercepted in the fifth house sends a square. Apart from the strong influence they possess as rulers of the ninth, tenth, and eleventh houses, Uranus is particularly significant for showing the sexuality to be homosexual and feminine. The femininity is pathological as Venus is also ruler of the house on the sixth cusp of illness and is dispositor of the retrograde Mars located in the twelfth house and in an intercepted sign! These two intercepted planets in the fifth house send aspects into the twelfth house—that is, Uranus is trine Neptune retrograde (while the latter is in opposition to Mercury intercepted in the sixth), and Venus is trine the retrograde Mars, suggesting not only sadism but the use of drugs.

The first impression the native gave was one of false joviality, due to the Sun trine Jupiter retrograde in the house of friendships, but Jupiter also has a wide square from the retrograde Mars intercepted in the twelfth house; Jupiter is also ruler of both the house of partnerships and the house of death! The feelings—the Moon—are of no help, nor is the intellect, as the Moon is located in an intercepted sign in the eleventh house and is spoiled by the sick personality (Moon trine Mercury, the horoscope ruler; Moon sextile retrograde Neptune in the twelfth house).

His ultimate fate is shown by Saturn and the retrograde Mars adversely aspecting the retrograde Jupiter, ruler of the house of death. Mars also reveals his disturbed sexuality as it is retrograde and trine Venus intercepted in the fifth but ruler of the sixth. The Sun, ruler of the fifth and intercepted in the sixth house is less powerful than Saturn, ruler of the eleventh and located at the cusp of the twelfth.

Uranus, whose importance we have seen to be increased by its square to the Ascendant, shows the complete commitment to homosexuality, while Uranus trine Neptune brings this retrograde Neptune further into the picture (it is already in opposition to the horoscope ruler). Neptune's rulership over the eleventh house while at the same time actually posited in the twelfth house of secret failings and enemies is typical for narcotics addiction.

This is the third time we have found Uranus in the fifth house and in an intercepted sign as well. The concepts "intercepted" and "retrograde" are from the psychological viewpoint—or better, from the psychoanalytical viewpoint—to be seen as indications of neurosis or repression.

Figure 6

For the sexuality of the native in Figure 6, Uranus at the cusp of the fifth house seems particularly significant, the more so as it has a close trine with the Ascendant. Uranus is conjunct Venus—a significant aspect—and not particularly favorable, since Venus shows certain attitudes the native has toward money by its square to Mars in the second house. Its action is also unfavorable through being placed in the intercepted sign Capricorn, where it becomes secretive and the final results will be neurotic since Saturn, its dispositor, is located in the sixth house and is in semi-square to Venus.

The ruler of the fifth is Jupiter, placed in the Jupiter decanate of Aries, but it is retrograde and conjunct the Moon, which in turn rules Neptune intercepted in the eleventh house. Mercury, ruler of the eleventh house, is in exile in the fourth and also has

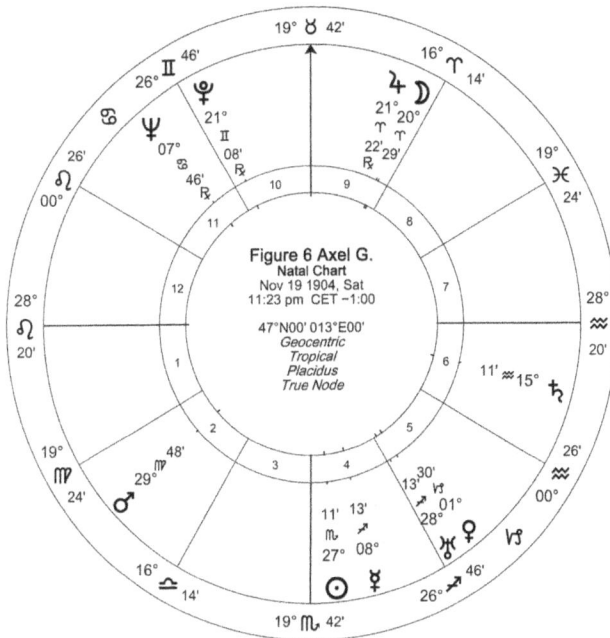

Figure 6 Axel G.
Natal Chart
Nov 19 1904, Sat
11:23 pm CET −1:00

47°N00' 013°E00'
Geocentric
Tropical
Placidus
True Node

this Jupiter as its dispositor. In addition to a quincunx to Neptune, Mercury has an important parallel with Uranus.

The Moon ruling Cancer and conjunct Jupiter in the ninth house, and Saturn ruling Capricorn and located in the sixth should be given special study on account of these signs being intercepted in the eleventh and fifth houses.

As the Descendant is in Aquarius, the cold, paralyzing influence of Saturn will make itself felt in the area of partnerships. Mars is important and unfavorable—not only does this planet square Venus but it also squares Uranus, suggesting a sadistic element. Mars is also strong through its sextile to the Sun in Scorpio. The fact that Mars is ruler of both the ninth and the fourth is, from the psychoanalytic point of view, evidence of the so-called "castration complex" and the aspect with Venus describes passivity and inhibitions. Inhibitions are also seen through the retrograde Jupiter in the ninth and its conjunction to the Moon, which in turn rules over the retrograde Neptune intercepted in Cancer in the eleventh, providing an additional impulse towards homosexuality.

We can recognize then a heightened sensitivity along these lines, which was not at all evident on the surface due to the tendency to lock this area off through the effect of Saturn. From all this one must assume there is an obstacle to the overt manifestation of the strongly shown homosexual components which, however, will have some neurotic effect in any case.

The native was a thin, somewhat feminine young man, who in regard to sex considered himself completely normal; even the possibility of admitting that a homosexual component of some sort is standard in every man was met with strenuous resistance. But in this case, what we feel to be established through astrology was indirectly supported during the analysis by an interesting occurrence.

A. G. was on an outing with a friend and because of lack of shelter both had to sleep in the same bed one night. The following night, when the friend was sleeping alone, the friend woke up in a cold sweat finding himself on top of a table in the room and saying that he had had a terrible dream that he was pursued by snakes. He went back to bed and tried as best he could to keep to the edge of one side of the bed. This friend of A. G. had no understanding of dream symbols and was embarrassed later when he confessed that the length of the snakes he was fleeing was 12 to 15 cm. He denied any understanding of what was presumably to be gathered in the situation. The effect of this dream was too strong not to have been conditioned by something occurring the night before. One must assume that it was a case of unconscious disturbances during the sleep of A. G. the previous night working on the friend's subconscious and coming to the surface during his dream activity—disturbances that are completely understandable through the horoscope.

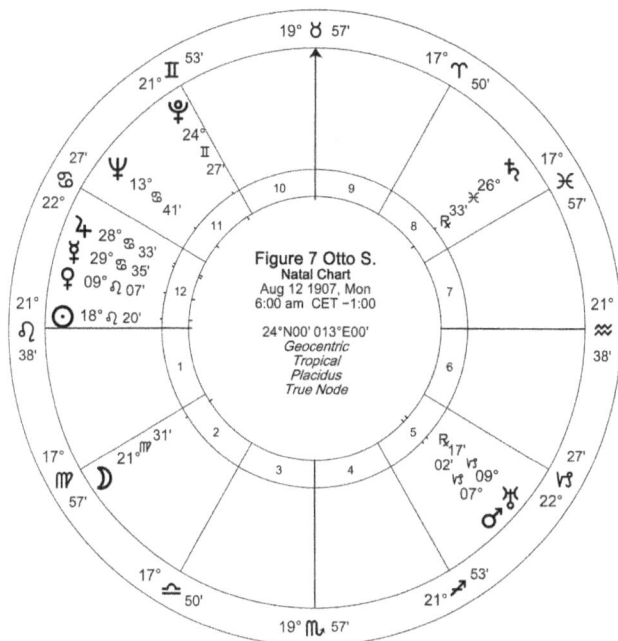

Figure 7

Figure 7 is in many ways similar to the preceding one, but in the dynamics of the configurations there is still considerable difference. Figure 7 is 2.75 years older than Figure 6, but the distribution of the house cusps is very similar.

The ruler of the fifth house of sex and love is again Jupiter, and again this planet has some relationship to the ruler of the eleventh; in the preceding case Jupiter was dispositor of the eleventh house ruler, while here the rulers of the two houses are in conjunction. This conjunction is located at the cusp of the twelfth house, which works unfavorably on both partners of the conjunction, but the situation is somewhat better for Jupiter and for the fifth house, as this planet is in its exaltation. Jupiter has three aspects, among which is a trine from Saturn.

A Saturn aspect to the ruler of the fifth house (and in this case to the ruler of the eleventh as well) is almost always crippling and damaging, even when the aspect of Saturn is relatively favorable as a trine would be, but in this case Saturn is not only in the eighth house and retrograde, but, just as in the preceding case, it is ruler of the sixth house of illness and the seventh of partnerships. More particularly, Saturn rules over the planets Mars and Uranus retrograde in the sign Capricorn, which occupies almost the whole of the fifth house.

As stated, Jupiter is conjunct Mercury, which planet is significant here through its close parallel with Venus in the twelfth house and its rulership of the sign on the eleventh house of friendships as well as the Moon in Virgo. Thirdly, Jupiter is sextile the Moon. But the Moon is ruler of Cancer which occupies almost all of the eleventh house and lies over the cusp of the twelfth.

Neptune, in this case direct, is in the eleventh house in Cancer and opposed to the retrograde Uranus. Neptune rules over Saturn in Pisces, and this latter planet is not only the ruler of Uranus but itself has an opposition to the Moon.

Venus in the twelfth gives us an idea how things will work out. As a result of very minimal sexual and emotional needs, which moreover are severely blocked by attitudes related to family and upbringing (Mars, ruler of the fourth and ninth, is conjunct the retrograde Uranus in the fifth), women and love affairs are unnecessary for him. He may even be impotent. The indications are of a strongly active, but repressed, neurosis.

The native was the son of a typical old Prussian military family with secure position and some sophistication. Although he himself had never been in the army, the influence of the military was always upon him. Traveling and intellectual interests were for him an apparent substitute for sex and eros, without his knowing—needless to say—that they were a substitution. On the surface of things he seems and is probably asexual.

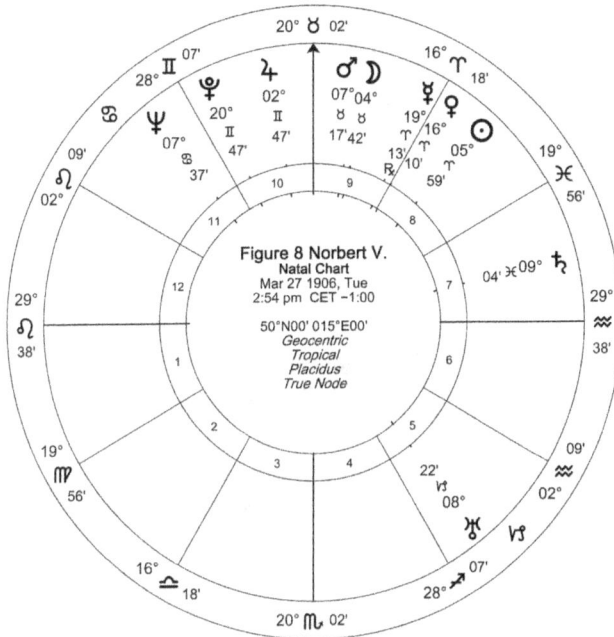

Figure 8

Figure 8 is yet another chart with the Ascendant in the third decanate of Leo and with Uranus in the fifth house and Neptune in the eleventh. While in Figure 6, Neptune was retrograde and in an intercepted sign, and in Figure 7 in forward motion but in opposition to Uranus, that planet here is again in an intercepted sign, as is also the fifth house Uranus. In the previous case Uranus was not intercepted but it was retrograde. Before we consider these planets located in the fifth and eleventh and in intercepted signs, let us take a look at the rulers of these two houses.

Once again the ruler of the fifth house is Jupiter—in exile but located in the tenth house; on one level such a location of the planet shows the opportunity of a sublimation of the sexual energies into career and status. Its dispositor is Mercury, ruler of the house of friendship and retrograde at the cusp of the ninth house. The planet's position in this house is in my opinion a sign of inhibition. There might also be an eros factor present, but that is hindered by the conjunction of Mercury with Venus, in exile and ruling the third house of practical intellect and the tenth of status, where Jupiter is located and semi-square to Venus. Mercury is conjunct the Moon, the latter ruling over Neptune, which is intercepted in the lunar sign.

Neptune gains in importance by its square to the Sun, the horoscope ruler. Neptune is also trine Saturn in the seventh house, the latter planet ruling over the same houses as in Figures 6 and 7, and here semi-square the Moon and sextile Mars and Uranus. Mars is trine Uranus, but the fact it is in exile diminishes the positive value of the strongly tenanted ninth house. Mars is ruler of the fourth house, so problems with respect to the parents are to be anticipated.

But the Sun, which is the horoscope ruler, is posited in the eighth house and is square to both Uranus and Neptune in intercepted signs. In addition, it is sextile Jupiter in exile, which suggests that the sublimation mentioned above is not quite attainable, and furthermore there is a semi-sextile to Mars. From these facts we feel the native will commit suicide. Love of friends appears strongly shown in this case but given some kind of neurotic expression.

It is felt that when a difficult period arises—probably concerning the collapse of ideals which are illusory, and aggravated by some conflict with the family—the critical effects of Uranus will come into play. In this case, the means of suicide would in all probability be pills.

The native was an "athlete with a child's personality" as someone once described him to me, and was forever busy "rescuing" prostitutes from their calling. To the psychoanalyst this kind of "bordello complex" is considered a strong indication of a latent homosexual component.

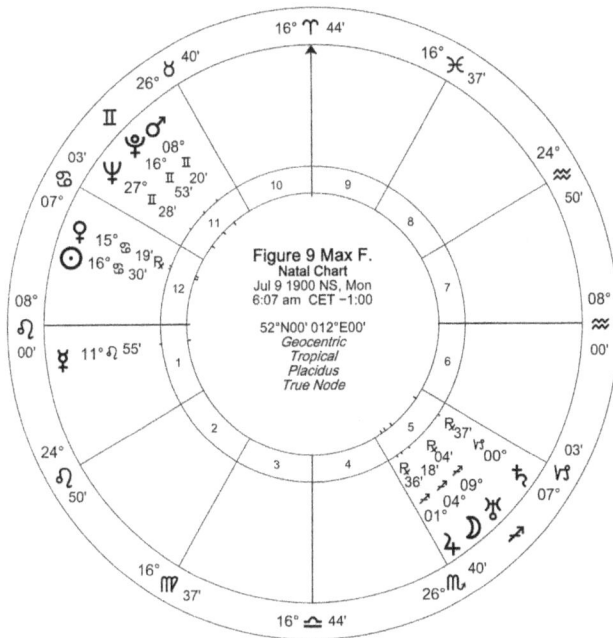

Figure 9

Once again (Figure 9) we have Uranus retrograde in the fifth house. The native has Mars, ruler of the fifth, in the eleventh house (the typical indication of inversion). It is not in exile but forms an opposition to Uranus as well as an opposition and close parallel to the Moon, ruler of the twelfth house of weaknesses. Moreover, the Moon is conjunct Jupiter in domicile, though intercepted and retrograde; Jupiter is also ruler of the ninth house of neurotic inhibitions!

Uranus has a trine with the Ascendant, while the Sun, ruler of the horoscope, is in the twelfth house and conjunct the ruler of the eleventh—both of these are indications underscoring homosexuality. Venus, in addition to being unfavorably placed by house, is also retrograde. The sign Cancer, and the Moon as well, gain in importance through these placements; the Moon is intercepted, is ruler of the twelfth, and is conjunct Uranus, which in turn is ruler of the seventh and eighth houses. The Moon is also opposed to Mars, ruler of the fifth and the tenth but located in the eleventh house. All these positions show a tendency to withdrawal resulting from feelings of inferiority and some neurotic factor at work in the area of friendships; this interpretation is supported by the Sun in Cancer and in the twelfth while at the same time horoscope ruler.

Also, the ruler of the sign intercepted in the eleventh house is in the first and conjunct the Ascendant and has a trine to the very significant Uranus, a sextile to Mars and a semi-square to Neptune which is moving toward the twelfth house.

Saturn's position and rulership incline to a tendency to isolation and to chronic illnesses, which appeared to be tubercular. Its opposition to Neptune signified the native's problem with drinking "so as not to be alone," as he himself stated. The bouts with alcoholism alternated with the native's injecting morphine.

And here once again I can only mention the many references in psychoanalytic and psychiatric literature to the effect that the tendency to inject narcotics has a clearly discernible relation to a homosexual component in the personality.

Figure 10

In Figure 10, Uranus is once again in the fifth house, but neither retrograde nor in an intercepted sign; it forms a wide conjunction with the ruler of the Ascendant. Furthermore, the Sun is square Jupiter, ruler of both the fifth house and the eighth and placed in its own sign Pisces in the eighth; this means a strong tendency to non-materialization of fifth house affairs. Jupiter is also semi-square Mars, ruler of the fourth and ninth houses and posited in the sixth house of illness. It is also the dispositor of Venus in exile and in square to this planet as well; difficulties in family relationships are to be expected.

In considering the eleventh house of friendship it is striking

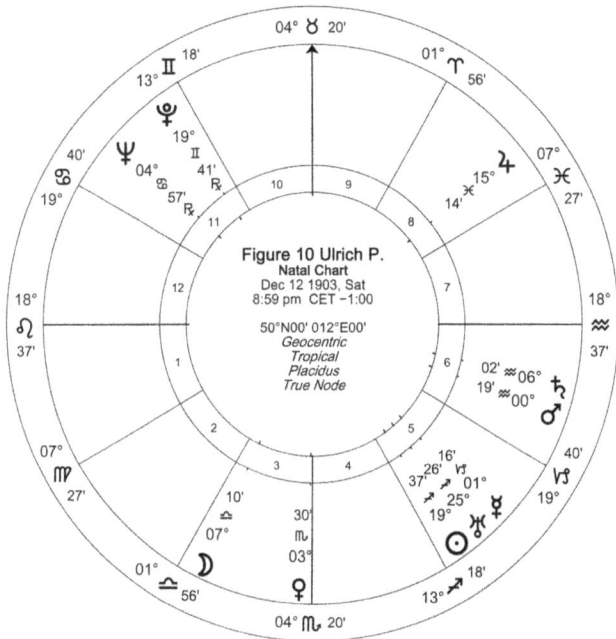

Figure 10 Ulrich P.
Natal Chart
Dec 12 1903, Sat
8:59 pm CET −1:00

50°N00' 012°E00'
Geocentric
Tropical
Placidus
True Node

that the ruler of the sign there is peregrine in the fifth house and in fact is in a rather wide conjunction with Uranus. The ruler of the eleventh in the fifth indicates that eros factors will appear in the sexuality—that eros is of considerable importance in the love life and that a certain inversion has taken place (see Figures 6 and 8, where the situation is reversed).

Negative elements in this case of homosexuality are unmistakable: Mercury, ruler of the eleventh, receives an opposition from Neptune in the eleventh, which in turn is square the Moon at the cusp of the third house of brothers and sisters (the Moon rules the sign on the twelfth house) and is also trine to the Venus in exile at the cusp of the fourth house. Finally, Saturn is trine the Moon but square Venus and is located in the sixth house while ruling the sixth and the seventh. These positions have an unfavorable result and tend to isolation, while Aquarius on the Descendant gives to Uranus an added importance.

Homosexuality in the Horoscope   71

The native has strong erotic feelings toward his friends but with maximum sublimation.

Figure 11

In Figure 11 all the planets are below the horizon with the exception of the retrograde Neptune in the eleventh house. This planet, with all its negative effects such as the danger of unrestrained imagination and self-deception, has an opposition from Saturn, in domicile and ruler of the house of illness. Its closest aspect, however, is the parallel to Uranus; the latter planet is at the cusp of the fifth house. And Uranus, as ruler over the sign on the Descendant and in trine to the Ascendant, became the symbol of the focal point of his life. The Sun is also at the cusp of the fifth house and acquires an impulsive streak through its square to Mars.

The fifth house is emphasized in a third way through the presence of Jupiter in domicile. But this Jupiter is also the ruler of the eighth house and the ninth house of neurotic inhibitions. Its closest aspect is the parallel to Saturn, although there is also a parallel to Uranus within an acceptable orb, and there is, of course, a wide conjunction between Uranus and Jupiter. Jupiter is also parallel Neptune. Saturn is also strong as it too is located in the fifth house and in domicile, while at the same time ruling over the sixth house of illness as well as the seventh. Its aspects taken together are unfavorable. It is made more impulsive by the trine to Mars, it supports the negative influence of the retrograde Neptune through an opposition, and it is in aspect to Venus, albeit through a semi-sextile. Perhaps this impulsivity is an unfortunate by-product of the native's heredity as Scorpio is intercepted in the fourth house.

In Scorpio we find Mercury, which is ruler of the house of friendships as well as the second and third houses. Its square to the Ascendant is significant, and it carries a sextile to the Moon in fall in Capricorn on the cusp of the sixth house. Saturn is

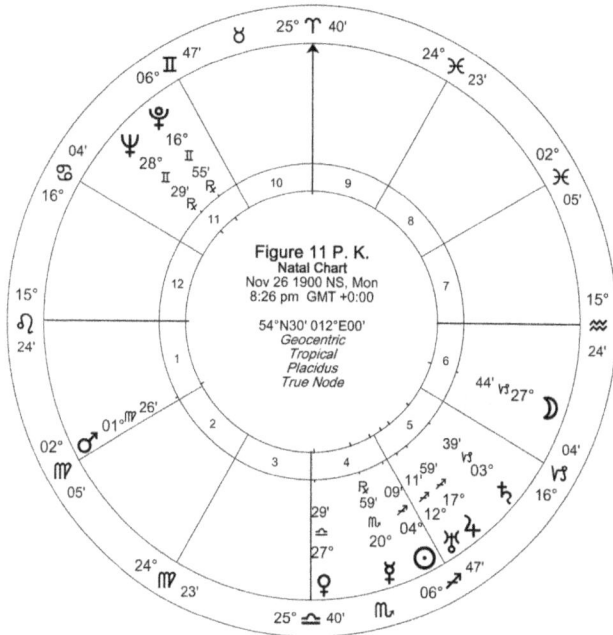

Figure 11 P. K.
Natal Chart
Nov 26 1900 NS, Mon
8:26 pm GMT +0:00

54°N30' 012°E00'
Geocentric
Tropical
Placidus
True Node

of course its dispositor, and the native is dangerously hypersensitive. The Moon is in an unfavorable cosmic state—in fall in Capricorn—in an unfortunate house, while the sign Cancer is on the cusp of the twelfth. Along with these positions and their meanings of moodiness and feelings of inferiority, the attitude toward women is further disturbed through the square of the Moon to Venus; Venus in domicile and conjunct the IC is in itself excellent though, from an analytic viewpoint, a mother fixation may be indicated since the square of the Moon to Venus is sufficient to introduce a neurotic factor and to produce disturbing effects.

The native's greatest pleasure was primarily in homosexual relations (Sun, Uranus) but he was carried away by emotional excesses (Neptune, Moon), driven to extreme reactions (Mars, Saturn), and his life ended in tragedy (Jupiter, Uranus conjunction Sun) when just past his twenty-third birthday he committed suicide. A "normal" student had played around with him and then dropped him, and he spent several weeks, including the Christmas holidays, in depression and feelings of loneliness; on January 10 he took three packets of veronal.

The native was more inclined to homosexuality than to heterosexuality but was by no means impotent in heterosexual relations! It was in friendships that he sought his "great love." He was smart to the point of genius, a hard worker, had a cultivated esthetic sense and was a decent, fair person though somewhat inclined to go to extremes. Some of the observations made at the autopsy report: "High forehead, somewhat irregularly formed, the left side is larger; the cranium has a strong slope towards the front. The top of the cranium was difficult to saw and is extraordinarily large and heavy, with no translucency."

The following astrological data are interesting: With death at twenty-three years, one month and fifteen days of age, the Ascendant had progressed on the day of death 0o18' Virgo and would have been conjunction Mars if it had reached that planet's natal position at 1o26' Virgo. Using the day-for-a-year method, on December 19, 1900, the progressed Moon was at 29o32' Scorpio and progressed Mars was square progressed Mercury. On the date of death, January 10, 1924, progressed Mercury retrograde was over the radical Moon, progressed Mercury was semi-square progressed Jupiter, progressed Neptune retrograde trine radix Jupiter, progressed Uranus quincunx Ascendant; progressed Sun at the cusp of the sixth house and semi-sextile Jupiter, progressed Moon conjunction progressed Uranus, and progressed Saturn sextile progressed Ascendant.

Figure 12

In Figure 12 the fifth and eleventh houses are untenanted except for Uranus, which is however already at the cusp of the sixth house. The native was one of my own psychoanalytical cases about whom I have already published some remarks elsewhere. It was a compulsive neurosis wherein imaginary hallucinatory

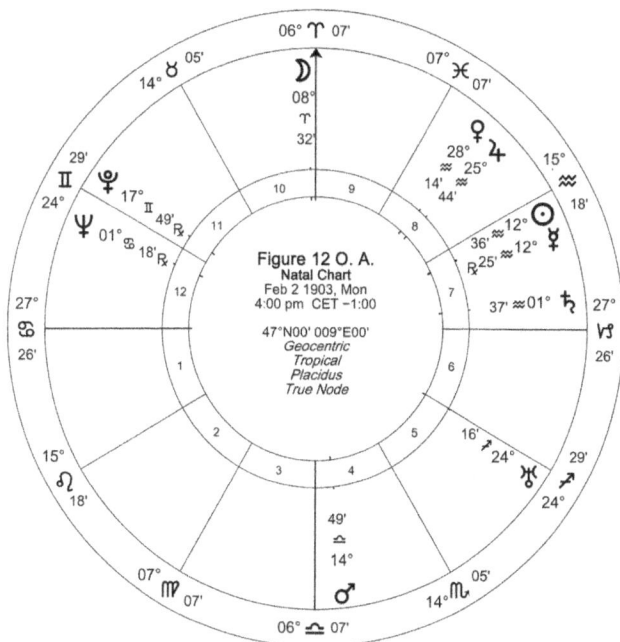

Figure 12 O. A.
Natal Chart
Feb 2 1903, Mon
4:00 pm CET −1:00

47°N00' 009°E00'
Geocentric
Tropical
Placidus
True Node

deformations of the face were seen, and these usually concerning his girlfriend; so, for example, her nose suddenly seemed to grow larger, and so forth. The analysis showed that a strong homosexual tendency was at work and was causing the neurosis. The trouble began with the death of the native's mother, so that the neurosis may be seen as a sort of penance or contrition.

Mars is ruler of the fifth house and is trine the conjunction of the Sun and Mercury on the cusp of the eighth, but is located in exile in the fourth house, and Venus, Mars's dispositor, is also in the eighth house and is ruler of the eleventh house as well. While the flaw lies more strongly in the heterosexuality, there exists for both components not only a tendency to non-materialization but at the same time a strong family fixation. Venus also has a trine to Neptune retrograde in the twelfth house, a sextile to Uranus at the cusp of the sixth, and a conjunction with Jupiter. This Jupiter is ruler of the sixth house of illness as well as the ninth, and is actually in the eighth house of death. It is also parallel Mercury retrograde and conjunct the Sun, as well as the ruler of the twelfth and third houses. This conjunction is sextile to the Moon. Saturn is powerful through its opposition to the Ascendant but has no other aspects.

The native was a charming, refined, artistic type of person (five planets in Aquarius) with whom it was extremely difficult to come into serious contact (Saturn on the Descendant); when he began analysis he was suicidal. The neurosis came to the surface when the Ascendant had progressed to the semi-square of the retrograde Neptune in the twelfth house, and during a Jupiter transit. The analysis went on for 18 months and a cure was finally effectuated, and this was one of my most difficult cases though it was successfully concluded. The latent homosexuality played the most important role but never became overt. In appearance the native seemed asexual. In this case the principal influence in causing the neurosis was Uranus on the cusp of the sixth house.

Figure 13

The native in case 13 was born five weeks later than the native of the previous case; the house cusps are somewhat similar. I introduce this horoscope in order to show that the position of Uranus in the sixth house of illness is by no means always connected with a homosexual neurosis—that is, a neurotic manifestation of homosexuality.

In this case both the ruler of the fifth and that of the eleventh house are in exile, and both are at the same time rulers of the signs intercepted in these houses; they are also connected by a parallel. Mars is ruler of the eleventh and the sign intercepted in the fifth but is located in the fourth house of parents and is retrograde; it has a square to the Ascendant and a trine to Mercury. Venus is ruler of the fifth and the sign intercepted in the eleventh and is in the tenth house in sextile to Saturn. The direction of the sexuality seems an open question.

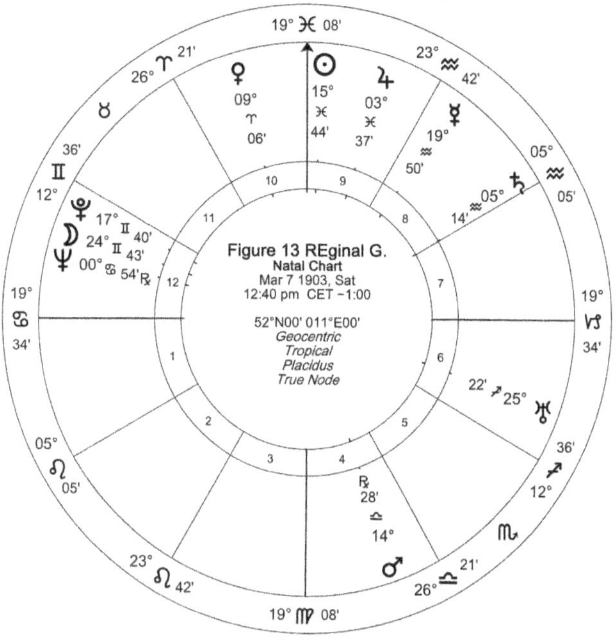

Figure 13 REginal G.
Natal Chart
Mar 7 1903, Sat
12:40 pm CET −1:00

52°N00' 011°E00'
Geocentric
Tropical
Placidus
True Node

In fact, the native is an extraordinary trance-medium. The horoscope ruler, the Moon, is in wide conjunction to Neptune, while Neptune's sign Pisces is on the Midheaven wherein the dominant Jupiter is found while actually in the ninth house; this Jupiter is in turn trine Neptune. On the other hand this Moon as well as Neptune have an opposition from Uranus.

The native is quite effeminate and is homosexual. Effeminacy is to be seen from the horoscope: The male planet Mars is retrograde and in exile in an air sign; Mercury and Jupiter are also in air signs; Jupiter is in its watery and passive domicile and, besides Uranus, only the exiled Venus is in a fire sign.

Figure 14

Uranus is on the Descendant in this chart of Christian W. (Figure 14), whose course of analysis I have described in detail elsewhere and published under the title "A Contribution to the Question of the Modification of the Active Method in the Therapy of Compulsive Neurosis—the Analysis of Christian W."

This was a case of a severe neurosis with compulsive ideas and suicidal tendencies. The neurosis began to form when the progressed Ascendant passed over the conjunction of the retrograde Neptune in the natal horoscope, then broke forth when the progressed Ascendant reached the trine to the Moon located near the cusp of the sixth house. Only with much difficulty was I able through treatment to take the patient through the period when the progressed Ascendant reached the opposition of natal Mars. But eventually there followed an improvement which I would classify as a cure. The case is significant in that I was concerned with only the neurosis and made no attempt to "cure" the overt homosexuality, which in my opinion is clearly shown through the constellation and is immovable.

The nature and the severity of the neurosis is to be seen from the sixth house; located therein is the Sun (with reference to the house of the parents through rulership), the Moon, and the horoscope ruler Mercury—all in the Mars sign Scorpio. Mercury in the sixth, however, is ruler of the fifth! Libra is intercepted in the fifth, and Venus in domicile there receives the unfavorable square from Neptune, the uplifting trine from the dominant Saturn, but also the very unfavorable square from Mars on the cusp of the 8th house. In addition Mars is ruler of the sign Aries intercepted in the eleventh house, and Scorpio on the cusp of the sixth, suggesting an unfavorable and perhaps dangerous result—sadism.

In contrast to the fifth house situation however, Jupiter, ruler of the eleventh house is in its own sign at the cusp of that house. But it should be noted that to this sign Pisces the retrograde Neptune must also be referred. The sign intercepted in the eleventh is ruled by the very unfavorable Mars already described. So there will not be a situation without conflict. Jupiter is also ruler of the house of partnerships. Women did not interest the native

Homosexuality as Constellation

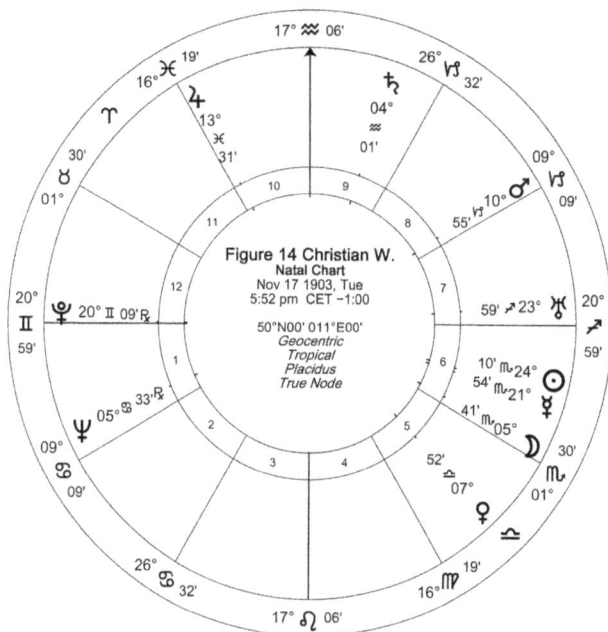

Figure 14 Christian W.
Natal Chart
Nov 17 1903, Tue
5:52 pm CET –1:00
50°N00' 011°E00'
Geocentric
Tropical
Placidus
True Node

much, and sexually they did not interest him at all. With such a constellation I was hardly able to do anything for this problem in therapy.

From the point of view of astrology I have serious concerns for the native's future: *Cave Martem!*

Figure 15

In the example shown in Figure 15 we find Cancer located in the fifth house, and in my experience this sign here is physically unfruitful for men; the Moon is in the first house, showing an egocentric concern over his own creative accomplishments.

This Moon is sextile the Sun, ruler of the sixth house, in the twelfth, indicating a too strongly individualistic character; Moon parallel Uranus brings self-will, while Moon opposition Mars, which is ruler of the horoscope and in the seventh, has

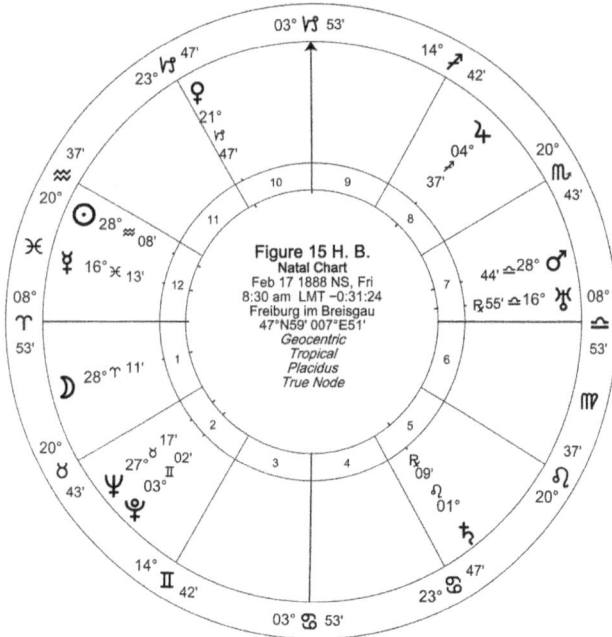

Figure 15 H. B.
Natal Chart
Feb 17 1888 NS, Fri
8:30 am LMT −0:31:24
Freiburg im Breisgau
47°N59' 007°E51'
Geocentric
Tropical
Placidus
True Node

brought him many enemies as well as unquestioning supporters and disciples (Mars is trine the Sun and square Saturn but its dispositor is Venus located at the cusp of the eleventh). The native's reputation has all the unpleasant disadvantages of sect and biased adherents; Moon has a wide square to Venus and is square Saturn as well.

As to the eleventh house, it is to be noted that Saturn, the cusp ruler, is in exile in the fifth house and is retrograde. Not only is the "inversion" factor to be considered but since Saturn is the ruler of the tenth, eleventh, and twelfth houses, the essentially prosaic character of his works is shown and, however, augmented in value by the trine to Saturn from the dominating Jupiter. The other aspects of Saturn have an upsetting effect: A square from the horoscope ruler in exile (personality), a square from the Moon (introverted sexuality), a sextile from Neptune, whose sign Pisces is intercepted in the twelfth house, and which in turn is square to the Sun actually in the twelfth house.

Of great significance is the opposition of the retrograde Uranus to the Ascendant, which, in spite of everything, has brought him his temporary but unquestionable popularity through the aspect with Venus, which is the dispositor of the exiled horoscope ruler and located at the cusp of the eleventh house, as well as his economic success as Venus is ruler of both the seventh and the second.

Neurotic elements are in evidence; there are some interesting things that the astrologer of sufficient experience can read for himself. The horoscope is that of Hans Bluher, the noted author of *The German Youth Movement as an Erotic Phenomenon* and *The Role of the Erotic in Male Society*, who holds astrology in the greatest contempt.

Figure 16

The chart shown in Figure 16 is complex with respect to sexuality. The ruler of the fifth house, at the same time the horoscope ruler, is in conjunction with the refined Venus in Aquarius in the tenth house. The Sun is also at the Midheaven but is in exile and its dispositor Jupiter is in the first house but retrograde as well as in exile; Jupiter is also ruler of the house of friendship and is trine Venus. Mercury has a parallel with Saturn, which along with Uranus, is intercepted in Scorpio in the sixth house of illness. Moreover, Neptune, ruler of the eleventh house, is retrograde in the twelfth house and conjunction the Ascendant.

As Jupiter is in wide conjunction with the Ascendant, and Neptune has a close trine to the Sun, the eleventh house affairs assume a significance at least as important as that of the fifth; Mercury ruling the fifth is in conjunction with Venus—an unfavorable position as the latter is ruler of the cusp of the sixth house as well as the sign Taurus intercepted in the twelfth house containing the exiled Mars, showing rage and latent sadism. The Moon is in its exaltation in Taurus and has a close opposition to

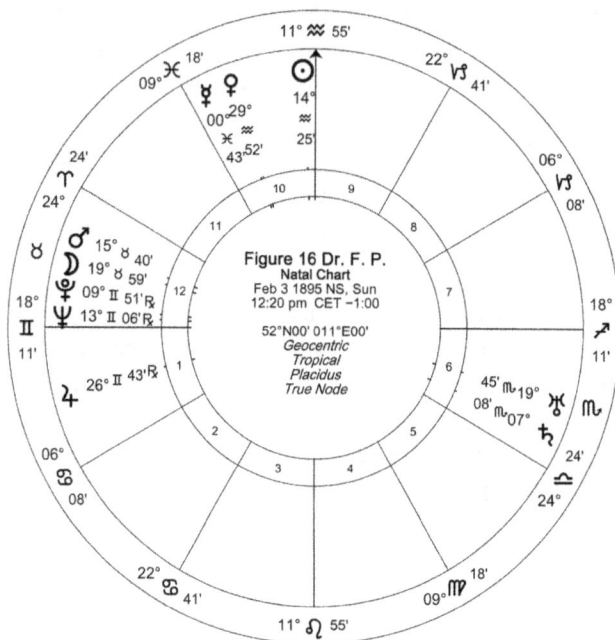

Figure 16 Dr. F. P.
Natal Chart
Feb 3 1895 NS, Sun
12:20 pm CET −1:00

52°N00′ 011″E00′
Geocentric
Tropical
Placidus
True Node

Uranus intercepted in Scorpio in the sixth, though outside the orb for a conjunction with Saturn also located there; the latter is parallel Mercury. These are all indications of neurosis.

The native is the author of several works of quite explosive character. He alternates between heterosexuality and the male eros.

***

The location of the ruler of the fifth house is of prime importance, as is also the position of Uranus. That Neptune also plays a very significant role can be shown by the many cases where Neptune is in the eleventh house of friendships. In such cases there is introduced a particularly hypersensitive and eccentric attitude so that disturbances easily arise in this area. Moreover, Neptune in the fifth house has just as disturbing and even psychotic an effect on the sexuality as does Uranus there. Though

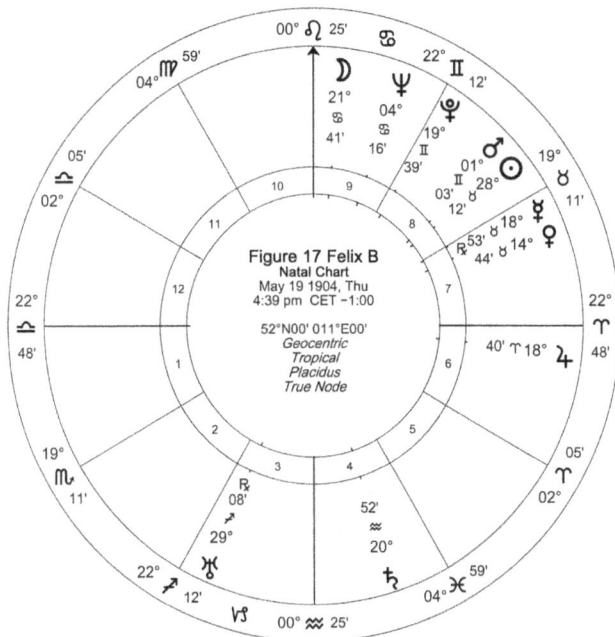

Figure 17 Felix B
Natal Chart
May 19 1904, Thu
4:39 pm CET −1:00

52°N00' 011°E00'
Geocentric
Tropical
Placidus
True Node

several examples have been given for the latter planet I have decided not to present a series of similar cases where Neptune is in the fifth house, and I will only mention that in such cases the accidental effects in the affairs of the opposite house played a significant and at the same time disturbing role: The natives always had false or fraudulent persons among their friends, and their friendships were often peculiar in some way.

There now follow six cases in which the ruler of the fifth house is connected with the Ascendant in some more or less negative way.

Figure 17

A very instructive case is the horoscope of Felix B. (Figure 17), whose personality was in no way suited to his given name. This was a case of a repressed homosexuality that seldom became overt.

There are no planets in either the eighth or eleventh house; the ruler of the fifth house is located in the sixth but is opposed to the Ascendant, while the ruler of the eleventh is retrograde and is at the cusp of the eighth house. In any case it is significant that the love of friends has won the upper hand, which is seen by the conjunction of Mercury ruling the eleventh house with Venus ruling the Ascendant and placed in domicile in Taurus, and perhaps by Neptune ruling the fifth but intercepted in the ninth; these positions indicate inhibitions to heterosexuality. The same is also shown by the sextile of the dominant Moon in the ninth house to the retrograde Mercury, and the tendency to non-materialization shown by the eighth house positions. Dangers lurk in connection with Mars in the eighth house which is conjunct the Sun and ruler of the second, seventh, and sixth houses. This is another case that shows a tendency to a violent outcome of the native's conflicts and problems.

Uranus sextile the Ascendant and Saturn trine the Ascendant say nothing specific with regard to sexuality. The native is of a very refined and high character with an aristocratic nature.

Figure 18

Figure 18 has the important feature of a grand trine of Mars, Saturn, and a retrograde Neptune—all in the second decanate of the water signs.

Again there is an interplay of the forces of the fifth and the eleventh houses; both are untenanted, but the Sun is placed at the cusp of the fifth and is ruler of the twelfth as well as in conjunction with Uranus. The Moon, ruler of the eleventh, is located at the cusp of the second house—with this house's tendency, in contrast to the eighth, to materialization. It is connected by square to the Jupiter in retrograde motion but in its exaltation and moving toward the cusp of the eleventh house; Jupiter rules the sign on the house of partnerships.

The horoscope ruler Mercury is in exile and has this Jupiter

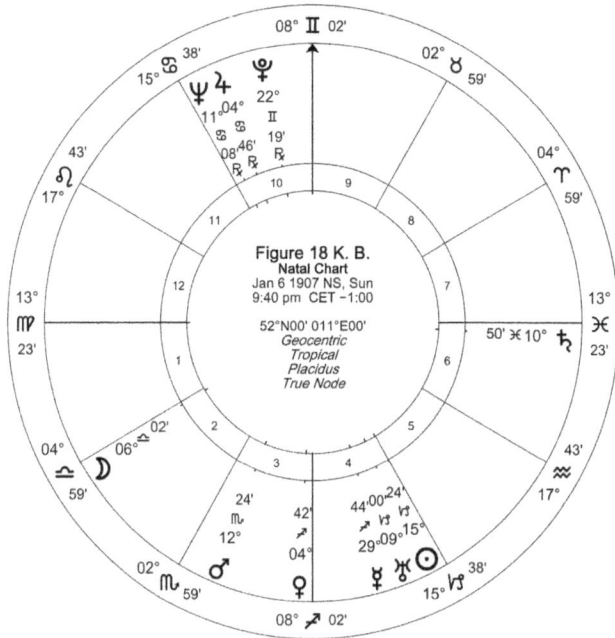

Figure 18 K. B.
Natal Chart
Jan 6 1907 NS, Sun
9:40 pm CET −1:00

52°N00′ 011°E00′
Geocentric
Tropical
Placidus
True Node

as its dispositor, which increases Jupiter's importance. Mercury semi-square Mars is an indication of some complex in connection with the native's brother, and this is shown further by Mars's important aspects—trine retrograde Neptune and Saturn in opposition to the Ascendant. One is reminded here of Figure 3.

The horoscope ruler's closest aspect is the parallel to Uranus, which is exact to the second, making this planet decisive; this position recalls the conjunction of the horoscope ruler with the ruler of the eleventh house in the preceding case. However, the ruler of the fifth house is in the sixth and in opposition to the Ascendant; this Saturn also has a link with Uranus through the sextile, so the heterosexual components are excluded—despite the retrograde Neptune, ruler of the seventh house, in company with the retrograde Jupiter near the cusp of the eleventh house.

In this case homosexuality was overt.

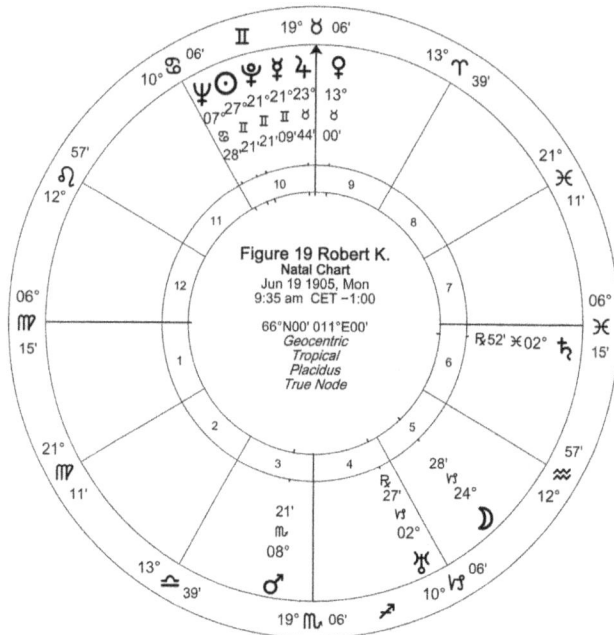

Figure 19

In Figure 19, Saturn, ruler of the fifth house, is vitiated by its placement in the sixth house and its retrograde motion, though it is accidentally strong by its opposition to the Ascendant. Saturn's only aspect is the sextile to Uranus, which is in the fourth house but fairly close to the cusp of the fifth. This Uranus is parallel Mercury, ruler of the horoscope and in domicile, as well as to the Sun. The Moon is ruler of the eleventh and is in the fifth, and Saturn is its dispositor; however, in my opinion the Moon in its exile is not so serious as when Mercury, Venus, Mars, Jupiter, or Saturn are in exile in any given case. The favorable trine and the parallel with Jupiter, which rules the house of partnerships, will cause this "inversion" factor to come into action.

Neptune, co-ruler of the sign on the seventh, is at the cusp of the eleventh house. At the cusp of the fifth house stands Ura-

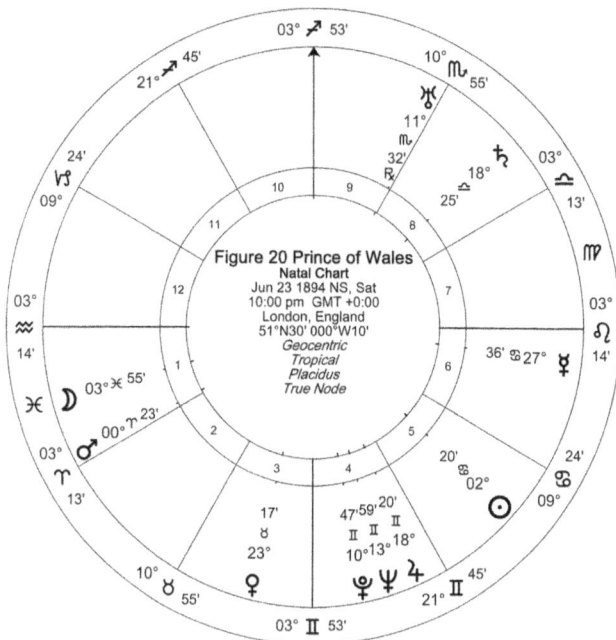

Figure 20 Prince of Wales
Natal Chart
Jun 23 1894 NS, Sat
10:00 pm GMT +0:00
London, England
51°N30' 000°W10'
Geocentric
Tropical
Placidus
True Node

nus, retrograde, in opposition and parallel the Sun, ruler of the twelfth, as well as parallel the horoscope ruler Mercury in domicile; Uranus is sextile to the retrograde Saturn in the sixth house.

The high level of the native's character is shown by the horoscope ruler in domicile in the tenth house in conjunction with the Sun, by the cusp of the third house lying in the last degree of esthetic Libra, whose ruler is also ruler of the tenth while placed in the ninth. The ninth house has the active sign Aries on its cusp and its ruler is in the third.

The native showed a not very active sexuality, of a primarily eros-type nature, but without any specific one-sided orientation.

Figure 20

The chart shown in Figure 20 is a difficult horoscope, and particularly so with respect to sexual matters. Once again the ruler of the fifth house is in a wide opposition to the Ascendant while located in the sixth house. In addition, the ruler of the eleventh house is not only placed close to the cusp of the fifth—we have noticed this several times already to be the indication of an "inversion"—but it is also in exile, and has Mercury, the ruler of the fifth house, as its dispositor.

The aspects of these two planets are as follows: Mercury has a trine from Mars in domicile on the cusp of the second house, a sextile from Venus also in domicile at the cusp of the third, and a parallel from Neptune. Jupiter has a trine with the horoscope ruler Saturn, while Saturn is exalted and on the cusp of the eighth house; Jupiter is also widely conjunct Neptune.

Since the cusp of the sixth house is in Cancer, and the afflicted Sun is drawing near to this cusp, while the Moon is intercepted in the first house, disturbances are to be expected from this source, and in part through the square of Mars. Again, the trine of the horoscope ruler, Saturn, to Jupiter will add to the significance of the affairs connected with these planets.

Uranus, which is retrograde on the cusp of the ninth house, gains in importance through its rulership of the rising sign, but works more toward inhibiting the native with respect to heterosexuality than it does toward furthering homosexuality; it has an exact parallel with the ruler of the fifth house as well as Mercury, the dispositor of the ruler of the eleventh. The fact that Uranus is the planet of greatest elevation adds further to its significance.

A brief examination of the seventh house shows nothing very specific in evidence, particularly in the light of what we know about the two determining components of sexuality, as well as the native's restricted opportunities. I should like to quote Raphael's interpretation:

> Regarding marriage the indications are conflicting. The Moon is arriving at a trine with the retrograde Uranus while the Sun, ruler of the seventh, has a square from Mars along with a trine to the Moon. These influ-

ences explain the fact that at the time of this writing (1924) the native is still unmarried. Venus reaches the conjunction with the Sun and the trine to the Moon only four years from now.

This is a nativity whose greater understanding requires the elucidation of further principles, and the horoscope should be considered in connection with the horoscope of the native's parents. For this reason I have given an analysis of these in chapter 9, where the problem of astrological heredity is considered. As far as the sexual orientation of the Prince of Wales is concerned, the rumors of his alleged homosexuality do seem to be justified. And after so many projects for his marriage have ended in failure it appears that he can no longer be counted on to produce successors.

(As is usually the case, hindsight makes the horoscope even more interesting and the reader will have no difficulty in tracing the native's famous abdication in the chart: Jupiter, ruler of the Midheaven, is in exile and conjunct Neptune in the fourth, showing the renunciation of an inherited position. Uranus, ruler of the Ascendant, on the cusp of the ninth certainly shows the long residences abroad while in exile from his native land. Saturn ruling the first and twelfth while in the eighth must show the burden of his "inheritance" but its exaltation in Libra and trine to Jupiter show it was not denied him (he did become king). The chart for the native's accession as Edward VIII shows Mars and Saturn in the fifth, further pointing up the difficulties in producing children or an heir. See Edward Lyndoe's comments on these charts in his *Complete Practical Astrology*.)

Figure 21

The horoscope in Figure 21 shows a certain similarity to that of the Prince of Wales. The ruler of the fifth house is again in opposition to the Ascendant, but in the seventh rather than the sixth house; it is, however, retrograde. It receives the exact trine of Mars located in its fall; Mars is conjunct Neptune and the

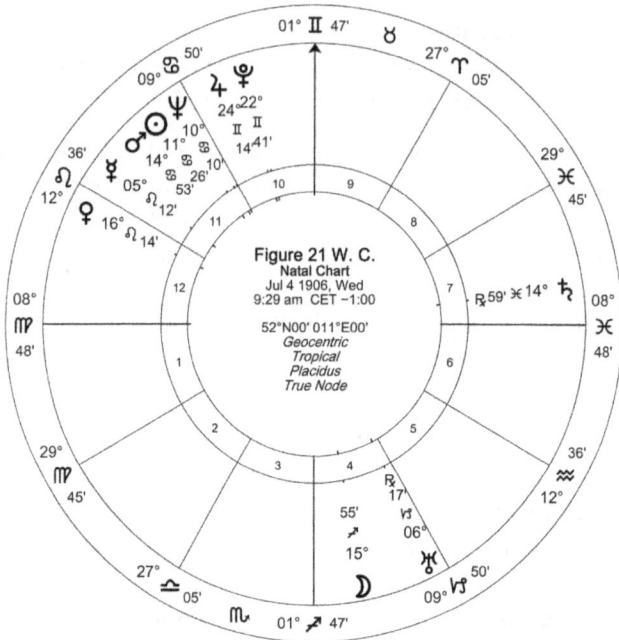

Figure 21 W. C.
Natal Chart
Jul 4 1906, Wed
9:29 am CET −1:00

52°N00' 011°E00'
Geocentric
Tropical
Placidus
True Node

Sun, has a close parallel with Uranus and is located in the eleventh house of friendships.

Furthermore, Saturn is square the Moon, ruler of the eleventh. Mercury, the horoscope ruler, is quincunx Uranus and in the eleventh: Uranus itself is retrograde and is at the cusp of the fifth house. Further neurotic elements are unmistakable: The retrograde Saturn is also ruler of the sixth and Uranus is co-ruler.

Jupiter, ruler of the house of partnerships, is in exile and has the horoscope ruler Mercury as its dispositor. Venus, which is at the cusp of the twelfth, has little to do with female partnerships and has a trine with the Moon in the fourth house; the Moon is also square Saturn, ruler of the fifth, indicating a mother fixation of unfavorable character.

Does the strongly tenanted eleventh house of friendships with the conjunction there of the Sun, Neptune, and Mars in fall, as well as Mercury the ruler of the horoscope, indicate an overwhelming inclination towards homosexuality? In any case, family relationships and partnerships will be spoiled by Jupiter (ruling both the fourth and the seventh) exiled in the tenth house, while partnerships are shown to be even more unfavorable by the conjunction of Neptune (co-ruler of the seventh) with the Sun ruling the twelfth house of secret weaknesses. The native will therefore be ruined through malicious and unreliable flatterers. Mars as ruler of the eighth house will create further troubles.

As good as this horoscope appears at superficial glance, the native will scarcely experience much good fortune in connection with his love life.

Figure 22

Again, in Figure 22, the ruler of the eleventh house is connected with the Ascendant; in this case Jupiter is in conjunction to it. Though this aspect is not particularly favorable since Jupiter is in fall, its influence is made stronger by Jupiter's conjunction with Saturn, the horoscope ruler. Mercury, ruler of the fifth house, is in exile in Pisces and is located at the cusp of the second house, while its sextile to its dispositor Jupiter is not wholly favorable. Jupiter is influenced further by its parallel to Uranus and the latter planet is retrograde in the eleventh house.

Unfortunately, there are even more neurotic factors. Uranus in the eleventh has an opposition to the Moon, which is drawing close to the cusp of the sixth and is ruler of the house of partnerships, while at the cusp of the sixth we find Neptune. Mercury is ruler of the fifth and in exile in Neptune's sign, while Venus, though exalted in Pisces, has the very unfavorable square to Neptune. Saturn, the horoscope ruler, is parallel Neptune.

It seems important to point out the fact that the male planets Mars and Uranus are retrograde, the male Jupiter is in fall, while Mercury—in this case feminine—is in exile and Venus

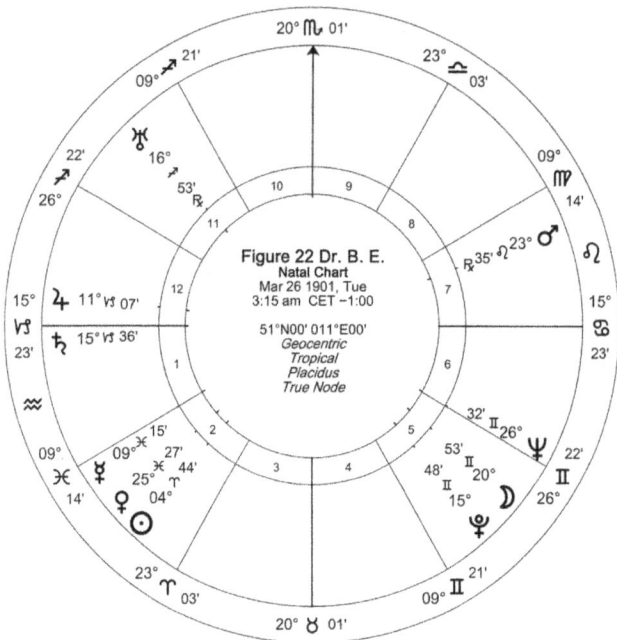

Figure 22 Dr. B. E.
Natal Chart
Mar 26 1901, Tue
3:15 am CET −1:00

51°N00' 011°E00'
Geocentric
Tropical
Placidus
True Node

is exalted; the native has a very delicate nature and is markedly feminine. Physically he is of middle stature, thin, dark, with a very beautiful face with quite sharp features.

It is one more case of the type of person who, like Hamlet, had no desire for either men or women. Neurotic characteristics are operating in a homosexual setting. He will probably go the route of that publicly acceptable method of prostitution-a marriage for money, as the ruler of the fifth house is at the cusp of the second. There is also a problem concerning alcohol and morphine, which he is able to obtain easily as he is a physician. But the native is a decent person though not robust, and in some ways rather infantile.

Figure 23

Once again, in Figure 23, the ruler of the eleventh house is in close conjunction with the Ascendant. The Moon is ruler of

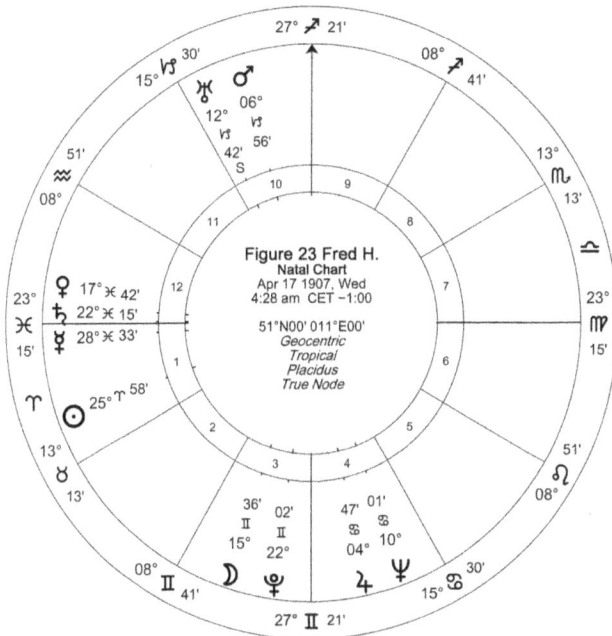

Figure 23 Fred H.
Natal Chart
Apr 17 1907, Wed
4:28 am CET -1:00

51°N00' 011°E00'
Geocentric
Tropical
Placidus
True Node

the fifth house and is at the cusp of the third, indicating a connection with a brother as a love object (the native had no sisters, only brothers). The Moon has a square from Venus exalted in the twelfth house and ruler of the second house as well of Libra intercepted in the seventh.

Feelings of inferiority further limit the heterosexual activity, if not completely prevent it. Not only is Cancer on the cusp of the fifth house, but Neptune is drawing near to that cusp and is in opposition to Uranus. Capricorn is on the cusp of the eleventh house and Uranus is near to the cusp; as already stated, Saturn ruling the eleventh is in close conjunction with the Ascendant.

Mercury, ruler of the seventh house, is in exile and located in the first house in wide conjunction with the Ascendant. Its dispositor, the horoscope ruler Jupiter, is located in the fourth house and has an opposition from Mars which in turn is ruler of the Sun-sign Aries, intercepted in the first house.

Homosexuality in the Horoscope   93

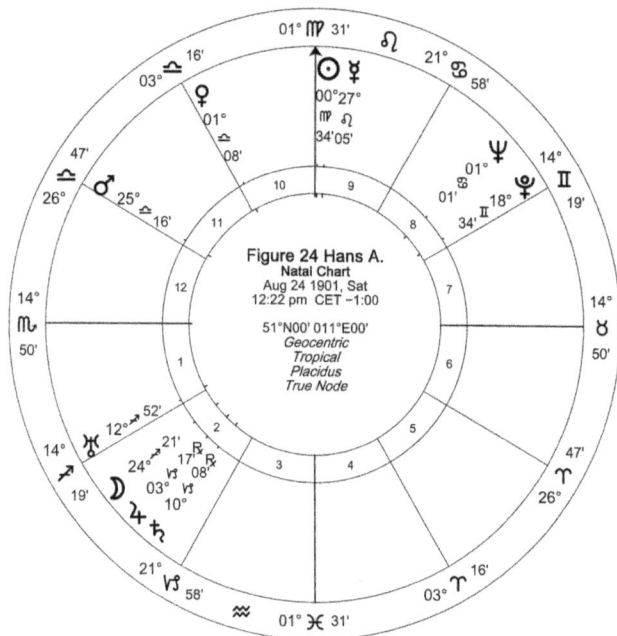

Figure 24 Hans A.
Natal Chart
Aug 24 1901, Sat
12:22 pm CET –1:00

51°N00' 011°E00'
Geocentric
Tropical
Placidus
True Node

With the exception of Jupiter and Neptune in the fourth house, only the eastern half of the horoscope is occupied. This, the Sun in the first house, and the fact that the horoscope ruler is the dispositor of the ruler of the seventh house of partnerships, result in a strong introversion, which, even more than the position of the ruler of the fifth house, is the basis for the native's homosexuality. I consider the location of the eleventh house ruler to be an even more decisive factor here than the planet Uranus.

The native, despite his gentleness, is a person of great energy and a true friend possessed of a really unusual altruism.

Figure 24

The man whose chart is Figure 24 is completely oriented to homosexuality. From the standpoint of astrology it is a particularly clear example of the dynamic interplay between heterosexual and homosexual forces.

The homosexual component is seen from the eleventh house where Libra is on the cusp and Venus is in domicile and located at the cusp of the eleventh. The heterosexual component is seen from the fifth house where Aries is on the cusp, and Mars ruler of the cusp is in exile and very severely weakened. Also, Venus, ruler of the eleventh, is Mars's dispositor; the heterosexual forces therefore find their expression in the love of friends.

However, as this ruler of the fifth house is unfavorably placed close to the cusp of the twelfth house and yet still located in the eleventh, its power is further transformed and an "inversion" takes place. At the same time, Venus ruling the eleventh house cusp is the dispositor of Mars, ruler of the rising sign, and this feature strengthens in importance those affairs referable to Venus.

In fact, Mars at the cusp of the twelfth house and in unfavorable cosmic state will have a marked effect on the general personality, but Venus will provide some compensation through its favorable state and position in the tenth house while drawing near to the cusp of the eleventh, and at the same time ruler of the seventh house of partnerships.

Other disturbing factors are quite significant; for example, the condition of the fourth house whose ruler Jupiter is in fall, and Neptune the co-ruler is in the eighth; their aspects are not favorable. However, these have externalized in the native's sex life only occasionally when there have been disturbing infatuations.

In chapter 8 I will analyze the horoscope of one of the partners of Hans A.

Figure 25

Dynamics similar to the previous case are found to be in operation in the chart shown in Figure 25. The Moon, ruler of the fifth house, is peregrine and therefore in a somewhat better cosmic state, but its position actually in the twelfth house is worse. The ruler of the eleventh house—in this case Saturn—is also in

Figure 25 J. K. B.
Natal Chart
Jul 5 1901 NS, Fri
10:36 pm CET –1:00

54°N00' 016°E00'
Geocentric
Tropical
Placidus
True Node

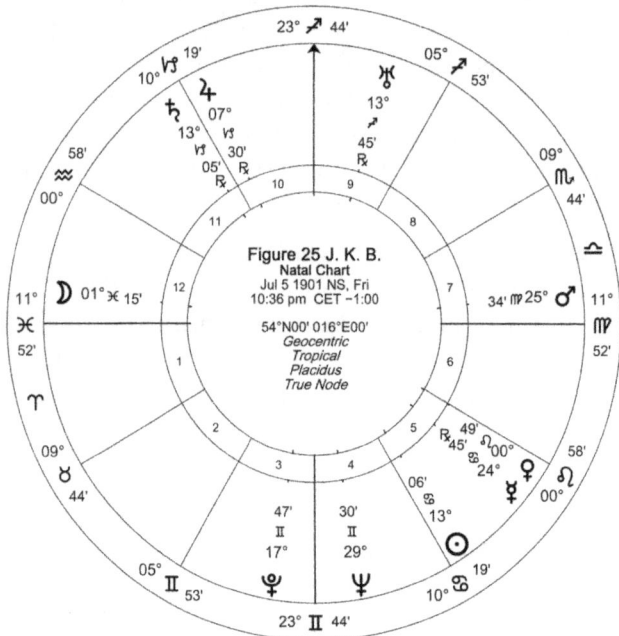

its own sign and at the cusp of the eleventh house, albeit retrograde in motion. Moon and Saturn are in semi-square; the latter planet is of course the stronger. Jupiter, ruler of the horoscope, retrograde and in fall at the cusp of the eleventh house lends further importance to the matters of this house.

The aspects of Neptune, co-ruler of the rising sign, are significant; placed in the fourth, this planet receives the trine of the Moon in the twelfth ruling the fifth, the parallel of Saturn ruling the eleventh and the semisquare of Venus located on the cusp of the sixth. The position of the Sun in Cancer strengthens the negative quality of the Moon. Uranus is the planet with the greatest elevation and has both a parallel and a semi-sextile to the eleventh house Saturn. Other neurotic factors I will not go into here.

The native is predominantly homosexual but feels no problem in this regard.

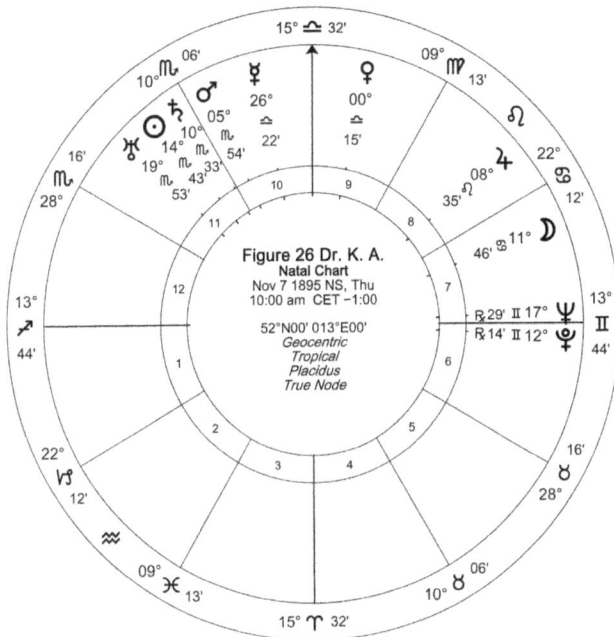

Figure 26

When the native whose chart is shown in Figure 26 began
analysis with me he was 100 percent homosexual and completely incapable of sexual and deep spiritual contact with women.
There had never before been a heterosexual orgasm. Involve-
ments were followed by terrible recriminations, suicidal tendencies, and rapid separations. There were many, seemingly totally
unselective relationships with homosexuals.

Only twenty days were at our disposal for the analysis and
in the thirteenth session I uncovered the following trauma from
the native's dreams: When the native was seven years old he had
played at deflowering a young girl of only five years of age, who
very soon after died of some unrelated cause. And this dead play-
mate prevented him from relating to women! An elder brother
also became the object of a fixation, and there were unpleasant
factors involving his father. From the standpoint of analysis only

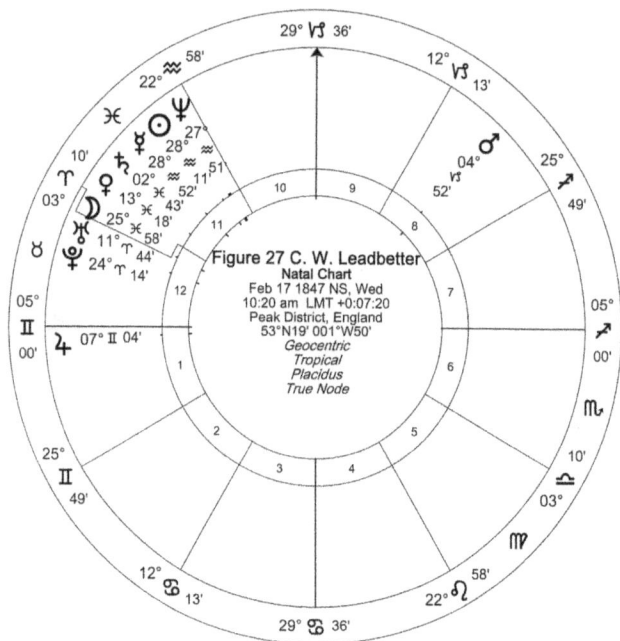

Figure 27 C. W. Leadbetter
Natal Chart
Feb 17 1847 NS, Wed
10:20 am LMT +0:07:20
Peak District, England
53°N19' 001°W50'
Geocentric
Tropical
Placidus
True Node

the "normal" bisexuality could be seen as a goal and would have to suffice. I felt that this was finally achieved and did not hear anything from him for one and a half years when I unexpectedly received an announcement of his engagement with no additional comment. (The analysis had taken place during the time when the Ascendant had progressed to 1o02' Capricorn.) The entire history of the analysis with all the important material has already been published by me as "The Analysis of Dr. K. A." in the *Annual for Advances in the Science of Sex and Psychoanalysis*, vol. 3, published in Vienna in 1928.

Venus, which is ruler of both the fifth and the sixth houses, is in good cosmic state as it is located in its domicile Libra in the ninth house and arriving near the Midheaven; it is sextile Jupiter, the horoscope ruler. There is an unfavorable semi-square from Uranus, which gains in power through its conjunction with the Sun.

The affairs of the eleventh house assume great importance through the three planets there. Mars, ruler of the eleventh, is unfavorable is its conjunction with Saturn, ruler of the second house (prostitution).

Jupiter, the horoscope ruler, is trine the Ascendant and is placed in Leo intercepted in the eighth house, whose ruler the Sun is conjunct Uranus. The role of the brother is also seen from Jupiter as ruler of the sign on the cusp of the third, while Neptune as co-ruler of the sign gives additional indications through its position in opposition to the Ascendant and in retrograde motion. Mars as ruler of the fourth house gives further indications of the role of the father.

Neurotic elements in the preponderant homosexuality are unmistakable, but the heterosexual components shown through the determinations of Venus are possible as well. So it was that in this particular case it was possible to promote heterosexuality through psychotherapy.

Figure 27

The horoscope shown in Figure 27 is one of the most unusual I have ever seen. At one time according to newspaper reports Leadbetter had made difficulties for his pupil Krishnamurti and the latter's attempt to gain entrance into the United States by apparently getting him in trouble with the British authorities, but the matter was finally settled before any appearance in court. But this episode can be taken as an out standing indication of Leadbetter's eros; but beyond this, I know nothing about what the man was or is sexually.

In the horoscope we find the Sun on the cusp of the eleventh house; the Sun is ruler of the fifth house and conjunct Mercury, the horoscope ruler, as well as the dispositor of Jupiter, ruler of the house of partnerships and located in conjunction with the Ascendant. The Sun is also conjunct Neptune and Saturn, the latter ruler of the eleventh house, peregrine, and posited in the

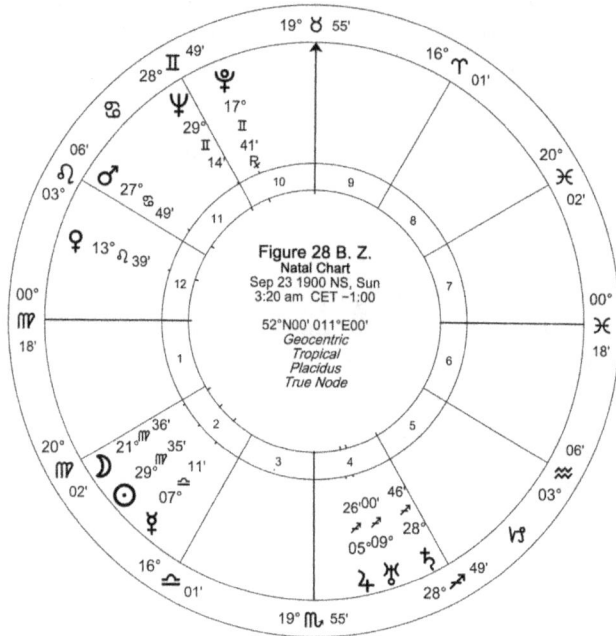

Figure 28 B. Z.
Natal Chart
Sep 23 1900 NS, Sun
3:20 am CET −1:00

52°N00′ 011°E00′
Geocentric
Tropical
Placidus
True Node

eleventh house in an intercepted sign. Venus and the Moon are likewise intercepted in the eleventh house.

An inhibitory factor is the semi-square of Uranus to the Sun and its conjunctions, its sextile to Jupiter in conjunction with the Ascendant, and its square to Mars located on the cusp of the ninth; the latter planet is ruler of the twelfth and sends a sextile to Venus intercepted in the eleventh.

I can only repeat that I have never seen a horoscope where there is such an overwhelming tenancy of the eleventh house, and where therefore the efforts and aspirations in the sphere of friendships must have been the focal point of the entire life.

Figure 28

With the chart shown in Figure 28 I want to pass to another group whose general feature is the limited role of an unsublimated sexuality. B. Z. spent his youth in a boarding school where

100   Homosexuality as Constellation

homosexual activities were forced upon him and is at present bisexual; while heterosexual orgasm is preferred, it is only men who interest him in a human way as partners. But every "love" is construed as something sick, or at the very least, an unpleasant and disturbing feature to his material ambitions.

Saturn is at the cusp of the fifth house and is the immediately unfavorable factor; it rules the sixth, as well as the sign intercepted in the fifth house. Saturn is opposed by Neptune at the cusp of the eleventh—unfavorable for friendships—while Neptune's ruler is the horoscope ruler Mercury, which in turn is located in the second house. The horoscope ruler Mercury has a sextile to the Jupiter-Uranus conjunction located in the fourth house; Jupiter is, however, ruler of the fifth, the seventh, and eighth houses. Incidentally, the native is an only child, and his father died while he was young. The mother-fixation is very strongly in evidence.

Uranus is parallel to Mars, which is intercepted in Cancer in the eleventh house and quincunx Saturn at the cusp of the fifth as well as semi-sextile Neptune at the cusp of the eleventh house. Neptune in turn is semi-square Venus in the twelfth house and square Sun in the second. The strong materialistic interests are seen from Sun and Moon in the second house, but because of the aspects involved it is doubtful if the native will have much success in this regard; Moon is ruler of the intercepted sign in the eleventh house, Sun rules the twelfth house and is square Saturn at the cusp of the fifth and Neptune at the cusp of the eleventh. The native will be taken in by deceptive and treacherous companions.

Figure 29

The native whose chart is shown in Figure 29 is another for whom sexuality plays an incidental and secondary role. Jupiter and Neptune—both rulers of the rising sign—located in the fourth are indications of a solid background and foundation in life, but also indicate a fixation on the parents; only exalted

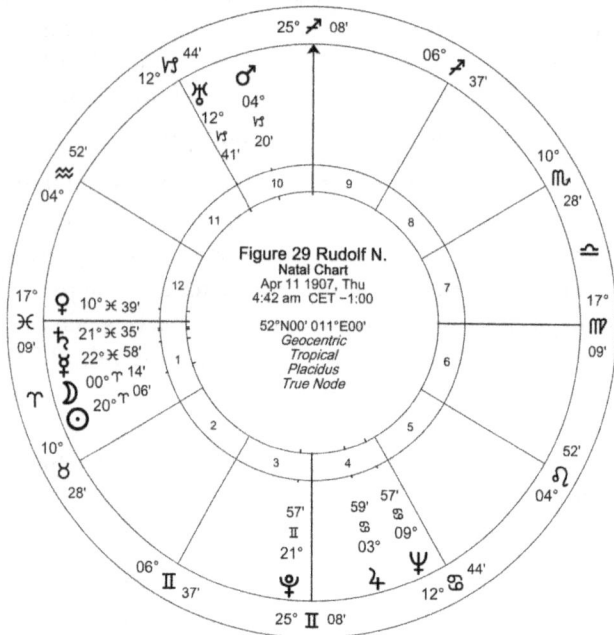

Figure 29 Rudolf N.
Natal Chart
Apr 11 1907, Thu
4:42 am CET −1:00

52°N00' 011°E00'
Geocentric
Tropical
Placidus
True Node

Mars, which stands in opposition to the likewise exalted horo-scope ruler Jupiter in the fourth, has the power to counteract this tendency. Neptune near the cusp of the fifth house trine Venus in the twelfth and opposition Uranus at the cusp of the eleventh seems highly significant.

The Moon rules the fifth house and stands in the rising sign and in the first house. This always causes a close connection be-tween strivings in love and the native himself—that is, a narcis-sistic or homophilic choice of love-object as well as a pronounced auto-eroticism. The Moon is square to Jupiter, which is ruler of the first, ninth, and tenth houses and located in the fourth house, and to Mars ruling Aries intercepted in the first house as well as the eighth; it is parallel to Mercury, which is ruler not only of the seventh but also of the third and the fourth; from these facts, as well as certain empirical information, a strong ten-dency to onanism with incestuous fantasies is to be assumed.

From the eleventh house it is clear that, because of Uranus on the cusp, there is a strong eros element also operating which cannot be considered positive. As the ruler of the eleventh house, Saturn, is in conjunction with the Ascendant, not only the affairs of the eleventh house gain in importance but the choice of friends becomes more oriented towards the native's own ego; that is, the choice is homophilic. The conjunction of this Saturn to Mercury introduces the fact that images of certain family members have been determinative.

The native is very much interested in gymnastics and sports. These interests cannot, however, be considered typical of Pisces, and from the point of view of psychoanalysis there is always a narcissistic and autoerotic tendency behind the pleasure in one's own body experienced in the pursuit of sports.

Figure 30

The individual whose chart is shown in Figure 30 is another case of the outwardly asexual type; the native, however, has strong eros feelings—but not sexual ones—for his male friends and occasionally engages in a self-demanding, forced heterosexuality.

Likewise there is a fixation on the parents but in this case it is not so clearly negative. The horoscope ruler, Jupiter, is indeed retrograde but is in a good cosmic state in its own decanate of Aries in the fourth house, and has an opposition to the Sun as well as a square to the Moon located at the cusp of the second house; there is a close trine to the rising Uranus.

Venus is the ruler of the fifth house and is located in exile in the eleventh, which introduces the problem of sex into the friendships.

Mars is ruler of the house of friendships, dispositor of the fifth house ruler, and located near the cusp of the ninth house, causing further inhibitions.

Joseph T. is an unusual young man in that he masturbated for

Figure 30 Joseph T.
Natal Chart
Oct 16 1904, Sun
11:50 am CET –1:00

52°N00' 011°E00'
Geocentric
Tropical
Placidus
True Node

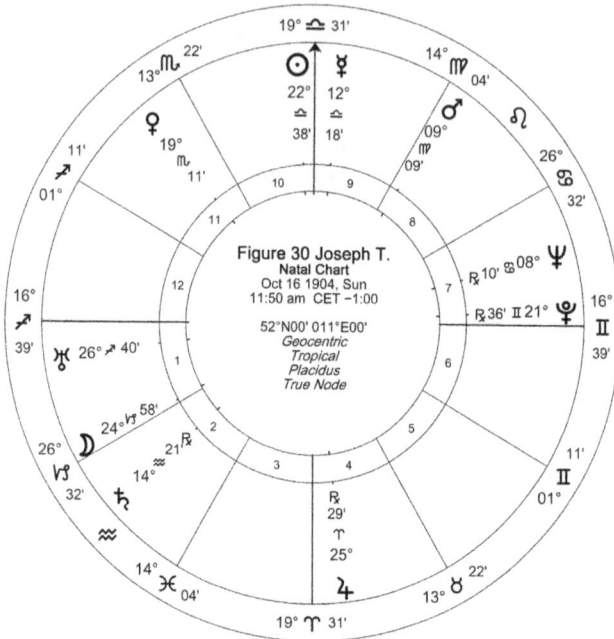

the first time at age twenty-one. Certain homosexual activities were more or less tolerated by the native when the progressed Ascendant opposed the seventh house Neptune. Moreover, the progressed Ascendant semi-square Venus allowed heterosexual activity to take place. His Uranus in the first house caused a singular power of attraction, however, and gave an unusual feature to his circle of friends and acquaintances.

Figure 31

The native whose chart is shown in Figure 31 is withdrawn from human contact in the extreme. The ruler of the fifth house is Jupiter, whose position at the Midheaven may be an indication of a sublimation, while the conjunction with the Moon in the ninth and ruler of the ninth seems to me to be inhibitory. In any case, the level of intellectuality and philosophical outlook is very high while at the same time narrow and closely defined. In-

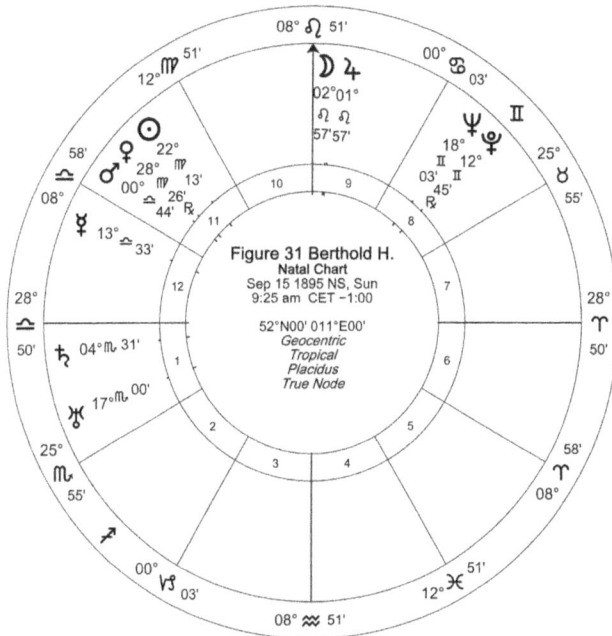

Figure 31 Berthold H.
Natal Chart
Sep 15 1895 NS, Sun
9:25 am CET −1:00

52°N00' 011°E00'
Geocentric
Tropical
Placidus
True Node

dividuality (Sun in the eleventh), personality (horoscope ruler in the eleventh), and partnerships (ruler of the Descendant in the eleventh) are all connected with friendships and eros-oriented, but as the ruler of the eleventh is at the cusp of the twelfth, these expectations have come to no fruition. The mutual reception of Mercury and Venus is significant since both could be taken as rulers of the horoscope.

His friendships are few. An unapproachable austerity blocks the way to him and the knowledge of just who he is can only be reached by a prospective partner with some difficulty. He cannot give himself. So, few people know anything about his human qualities since he does not obtrude himself and needs no one.

He is artistic and musical. Uranus in the first house is square the Sun in the eleventh, and the ruler of Aquarius lends here also the suggestion of the platonic eros. There is no trace of overt homosexuality.

Homosexuality in the Horoscope   105

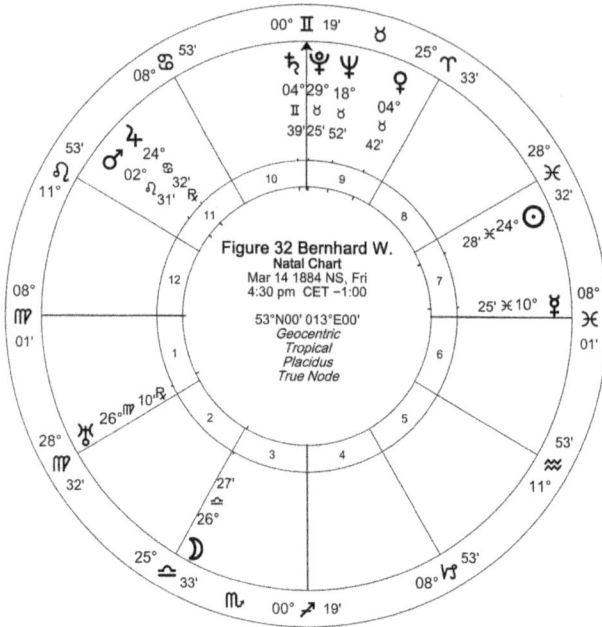

Figure 32

In Figure 32 we have another example of the sublimation of fifth house forces into the direction of status and profession by the ruler Saturn being placed at the cusp of the tenth house. The ruler of the eleventh house of friendships is the Moon, located at the cusp of the third house; it has a semi-square to Uranus and a square to Jupiter in the eleventh house. The horoscope ruler Mercury is on the Descendant and in close opposition to the Ascendant, and as Jupiter is its dispositor, the latter planet gains in importance by this fact as well as its trine to the Sun in the seventh house. Jupiter is retrograde but in its exaltation sign and sextile Uranus in the first house, while the latter planet's action is aggravated but somewhat impeded by the opposition of the Sun in the seventh, ruling the twelfth. The result is an almost completely sublimated heterosexuality combined with a strong homosexual component without this being able to become overt.

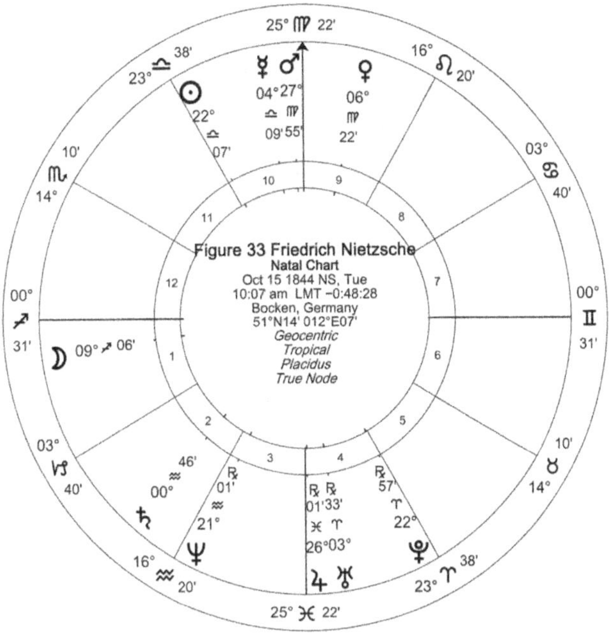

Figure 33 Friedrich Nietzsche
Natal Chart
Oct 15 1844 NS, Tue
10:07 am LMT −0:48:28
Bocken, Germany
51°N14' 012°E07'
Geocentric
Tropical
Placidus
True Node

The native is in the beginning of his forties and was for a time married though childless, and afterwards divorced. Body and soul were devoted to his profession and through his performance as well as certain important changes (Gemini in the tenth!) he attained considerable success. His inner life is completely absorbed with an exclusive circle of friends, and since the beginning of the war he has been interested in only four close friends. The native was an exceptionally fair, reliable, and aristocratic type whose sense of duty was exceptional and who had many diverse interests.

Figure 33

The last case (Figure 33) is that of the man who so contributed to the awakening of modern intellectual and spiritual life. Not only did the most refined concepts of eros originate with him but in all his work this eros characteristic is unmistakable.

Once again the ruler of the fifth house is in the Midheaven, and once again the antagonistic factors within the personality are not lacking: The horoscope ruler Jupiter, though retrograde, is in domicile in opposition to Mars at the Midheaven. Venus is the ruler of the eleventh house and is weak by sign in its fall and its position in the ninth house indicates a further sublimation of its values; it has a square from the Moon in the first house which in turn is ruler of the eighth, adding an additional factor of transposition and non-materialization.

The weak and neurotic remnants of sexual interest are homosexual. Mercury, ruler of the seventh house of partnerships and the Midheaven, is located in the tenth in opposition to the retrograde Uranus, while Venus in fall in the ninth and ruler of the eleventh is also ruler of the sixth house of illness.

Of course, from the point of view of analysis, one cannot miss Nietzsche's strongly expressed and considerable homosexual component (one thinks of his treatment of Wagner).

Chapter 6

SYNOPSIS OF HOMOSEXUALITY AND ASTROLOGY

Charles E. O. Carter writes in his *An Encyclopedia of Psychological Astrology*, under the section titled "Immorality (sexual)" dealing with sadism, incest, and perversions that the discovery of Uranus and Neptune has thrown much new light upon this subject. The afflictions of these planets "especially if affecting the fifth and seventh houses, invariably concern the morality and incline to irregular behavior." Homosexuality, a condition which is by no means always connected with vicious tendencies, "is nearly always referable to Uranus."

Oscar A. H. Schmitz in his book *The Spirit of Astrology* makes several observations on the general effects of Uranus, as well as a few more detailed interpretations—in part incorrect theoretically as well as factually. In any case, Schmitz emphasizes that "most dangerous of all is Uranus as a separating agent—causing estrangement in the relationship between the sexes. Thus in the seventh house he almost always leads to separation and divorce."

K. Frankenbach wrote in the March 1926 issue of his periodical *Man and Cosmos*, an article entitled "The Nature of Sexual Love and Indications of Homosexuality in the Horoscope," which was also published in Sindbad-Weiss's *Tectonics*, no. 3, and was one of the first attempts at a comprehensive statement, but he knew only the negative sides of homosexuality. After quoting Carter's remark that homosexuality is almost always referable to Uranus, he writes:

> This statement is doubtless correct, and I would only like to add that in the horoscopes of homosexuals aspects always occur between Uranus and a planet which is located on the ascendant, descendant, or the fifth house, or to the ruler of the first, seventh, fifth, or eleventh houses, and frequently to Venus. The actual location of Uranus on the Ascendant, Descendant, or in the fifth or eleventh house is not by itself any indication upon which the assumption of homosexuality could be based; such an assumption is justified when Uranus has an unfavorable aspect from one of these positions to a significator of the love life which is vitiated in its essential nature through its zodiacal position and aspects. Sexual deviations will be the more evident the more specifically the significators of sexual love are determined by zodiacal position.

However, I must state here that this concept—as I have tried to show in the range of examples given in the previous chapter—is too simplified and is not applicable in view of the complexity of the individual, not even in cases of overt homosexuality.

Moreover, male and female homosexuality are usually equated—that is, evaluated in the same fashion—and this is without question incorrect. I will give my own opinion on this matter in the next chapter as it is of basic significance.

Astrology is in fact a matter of combination and synthesis, while in its principles is indeed analytical. Just as in the interpretation of dreams in psychoanalysis, everything of importance follows from the specific details and individual references, in just the same way a Venus with unfavorable aspects does not in and of itself mean anything specific, and the various determinations of the planet are just as important here as the individual meanings of details are in searching for the correct interpretation of a dream.

All images of a dream have significance as specific elements of the dreamer—so goes an important psychoanalytical rule—an egocentric determination, as it were. And so in astrology we must likewise consider carefully every additional determination that may have significance. For example, many various meanings for Venus arise through its relationship to Libra and Taurus, as well as in general to the seventh and second houses: but many others related to the planet's accidental determinations must be considered as well. In a male horoscope one can through Venus find an indication of the man's softer, more passive side as well as of his financial capacity. His essential character will be shown by the horoscope ruler, which is always significant for the personality, and the Sun, which expresses individuality, and also by the masculine planets Jupiter, Mars, Saturn, Uranus, and perhaps Mercury. But it is quite different for women. While a bad Venus in a male horoscope indicates a hardness which will make his relationships with women difficult, such a Venus in a woman's horoscope represents the annihilation of her femininity.

But this cannot be considered completely sufficient, and one cannot therefore make the general statement that "Venus afflictions"—in particular the squares—are indicative of homosexuality.

Regarding the creative individual, for example, W. Fliess comments on the "extra plus of femininity" in the creative individual in his work *On Life and Death*:

> The more important and more frequent case is the one where there is apportioned to the individual an extra amount of the substance of destiny, and the superior man—the artist—is created. The male artist receives

beyond the normal measure yet a further admixture of femininity while the female artist receives yet an additional element of masculinity. This is why the artist—whether male or female—is an anomaly and even in his external appearance shows the added element of the opposite sex.

(One is reminded here of Figure 11, P. K., in the last chapter.) Fliess goes on to say:

> The artist is an anomaly and through his greater amount of elements of the opposite sex is not only capable of a higher performance but just because of this plus he can empathize more easily in all those situations which are the joy or despair of the opposite sex. Because of this plus he has received from nature the artist is able to give to his dream fantasies the strength of daylight and bring them to fruition in his work of art. For art as well as love arises from the tension between the sexes; man and woman embrace each other in the artist's soul, and the spirit of genius bears witness to that which makes him immortal.

In such horoscopes we would naturally expect to find a Venus that is outstanding, perhaps even indicating the receptive character of creative work through its position in the fifth house. But then we find also a "softer" element in the love life. The "femininity" of artists is well-known; well-known too is the higher incidence of homosexuality among them. But the connections here are of a secondary nature; they go beyond the complex of the "creative." But not only Venus is to be considered; F. Werle in his excellent work *The Horoscopes of Artists* quoted with justification the old motto *qui laborat sine venere et marte—stultus est in arte*. According to him the square is the aspect of tension, of the possibility of development, and therefore of the greatest positive value, and we should expect to find more Venus squares among creative individuals.

And again, the problem of the creative person is very closely connected with eros-with male homosexuality. So Uranus will then be strong as well as influential through its determinations for the spiritual nature of' the individual, and secondarily so that it may provide the basis of a "Uranian sexuality." Here also we should point out something that up to this time has been pointed out only by Werle in his book mentioned above—and that is *reception*. It is a connection which is far more fruitful for each planet than their conjunction would be, and the interpenetration of the two forces and planes is of very great importance. In the previous chapter one finds this reception in Figure 4 (Frederick the Great) with the Sun and Saturn, Mercury and Uranus; Figure 8, Mars and Venus; Figure 11, Mars and Mercury; Figure 13, Mars and Venus; Figure 16, Jupiter and Mercury; Figure 24, Sun and Venus; Figure 29, Moon and Jupiter; Figure 31, Mercury and Venus; Figure 33, Mercury and Venus. And it should always be emphasized that homosexuality or eros is also the expression of an intellectual and spiritual principle, and that the-creative man is less inclined to heterosexual reproduction. One has only to recall the very frequent childlessness of men of genius, or the fact that their descendants rapidly died out. As Mobius says: "Genius does not appear on earth in order to increase the number of human beings; its creative works are its immortal children."

As brought out in chapter 2, homosexuality is present in every man, but since it exists in a strong relationship to eros but not to sex the results for the one are an intellectual goal and for the other a physical one—that is, intellectual and physical reproduction. But for both, sexual foundations lie in common—both are "love." In the love of friends the physical element is means, not purpose; for the "normal" it is the other way around and the intellectual element in heterosexuality and marriage is means and not purpose. This possibility of intensification of friendship is these days proscribed by average public opinion; where it becomes or could become love it is judged as peculiar and even condemned officially through the use of terror. It is not allowed to operate as, for example, it did among the ancient Greeks. But psychoanalysis will almost always discover not only undeveloped rudiments of homosexuality but almost always some actual experience in this direction as well, just as it recognizes that the autoerotic or onanistic factor is never lacking. As Freud writes: "In the direction of homosexuality also the choice of object has been made beforehand." If homosexual activity, however, acquires the characteristics of love and is destined to be of significance in the individual's life it is then always evident in the horoscope, or at least to some extent through the directions.

In today's unnatural circumstances where there are heavy criminal penalties for homosexuality particular factors are required to lead the sexuality away from women and towards the love of friends—that is, in these days it is almost always a neurosis in heterosexual behavior which accounts for activities which deviate from the behavior sanctioned by the environment. Astrology fully supports our psychoanalytic observation that the degree of manifestation is in no way dependent upon the quantity of the latent element, but that the quality, the kind and the strength of the inhibition—the extent of the repression—are something completely individual, as are also the kind of reaction and related external events. And all are to be found in the horoscope.

The inhibition and tendency to repression that is known as the castration complex (whose meaning as constantly used by the orthodox Freudian school is erroneous in the opinion of W. Stekel) is something specifically individual, is constellational, and this conclusion is to be drawn from my several examples. I should emphasize here that I have used case histories of neurotic individuals and that this material is in no way representative of the average. I must continue to emphasize this fact to preclude the possibility of erroneous "statistical" conclusions being made from this material here alone. Homosexuality is not a "perversion" and is therefore not the "negative element of a neurosis"

(Freud) or even a neurosis (Stekel said: "Perversion is not the negative element of a neurosis, but a neurosis itself").

Now let us make some general evaluations of the preceding material.

Already in the distribution of the houses a difference becomes apparent: The eleventh house of friendships lies closer to the house of the ego—the first—than does the fifth house. Therefore, in contrast to the fifth house it is to be considered as having a more homophilic character. The affairs of the houses in the eastern half of the horoscope are all more introverted, or according to the orthodox analytical nomenclature, more narcissistic than are the houses of the western half. In the latter half lie the fifth house of love and sexuality as well as the seventh through which partnerships are fulfilled.

Planets in intercepted signs indicate factors which are latent or repressed, and through this repression present the danger of some neurotic transmutation as in Figure 1, twelfth house; Figure 2, eleventh house; Figure 3, fifth house; Figure 4, fifth, sixth houses; Figure 5, fifth, sixth, eleventh, twelfth houses; Figure 6, fifth, eleventh; Figure 8, fifth, eleventh; Figure 9, fifth, eleventh; Figure 11, fourth; Figure 14, fifth; Figure 15, twelfth; Figure 16, sixth, twelfth; Figure 17, ninth; Figure 19, tenth; Figure 20, tenth; Figure 22, seventh; Figure 23, first; Figure 24, ninth; Figure 26, eighth; Figure 27, eleventh; Figure 28, eleventh; Figure 29, first; Figure 30, second; Figure 31, eighth; Figure 32, ninth house.

Neuroses are most clearly seen from the sixth house as in Figure 3, the ruler of the eleventh, fourth houses; Figure 4, Neptune intercepted; Figure 5, horoscope ruler and Sun, ruler of the fifth, both intercepted; Figure 6, rulers of the fifth, sixth, eighth intercepted; Figure 10, rulers of the fourth, ninth, and ruler of the sixth, seventh; Figure 11, ruler of the twelfth and in exile; Figure 12, Uranus; Figure 13, Uranus; Figure 14, horoscope ruler and fifth house ruler, Sun ruling the fourth, and the ruler of the second, third; Figure 16, Uranus, and the ruler of the eighth, ninth, tenth intercepted; Figure 17, ruler of the third, fifth; Figure 18, ruler of the fifth, sixth; Figure 19, ruler of the fifth, sixth retrograde; Figure 20, ruler of the fifth, fourth, and an intercepted sign in the seventh; Figure 22, Neptune; Figure 25, ruler of the second and an intercepted sign in the seventh.

On the other hand, the twelfth house indicates an even deeper, more chronic, and abiding factor—more in the nature of a psychosis as in Figure 5—ruler of the ninth, tenth, eleventh retrograde, Neptune intercepted and retrograde, ruler of the twelfth in exile, retrograde, and intercepted, as well as ruler of sign intercepted in the sixth; Figure 7, ruler of the fifth, eighth, ruler of the eleventh, second, Venus ruler of the tenth, third, the horoscope ruler the Sun; Figure 12, Neptune retrograde; Figure 13, Neptune retrograde, the horoscope ruler; Figure 15, ruler of the third and the sign intercepted in the sixth; Figure 16, ruler of the twelfth intercepted and ruler of the sign intercepted in the sixth, ruler of the second, third, Neptune retrograde but conjunct the Ascendant; Figure 21, Venus ruler of the ninth; Figure 22, ruler of the eleventh, twelfth, second and conjunct the Ascendant; Figure 23, Venus ruler of the second and the sign intercepted in the seventh, but conjunct the Ascendant, ruler of the eleventh, twelfth; Figure 24, the ruler of the horoscope, the fifth, sixth; Figure 25, ruler of the fifth; Figure 26, ruler of the eighth; Figure 27, Uranus; Figure 28, Venus ruling the tenth, third; Figure 29, Venus ruler of the second and the sign intercepted in the seventh; Figure 31, ruler of the eleventh and the sign intercepted in the eighth containing Neptune ruler of the fifth.

Just as there is a difference between the sixth and twelfth houses in the relationship of neurosis to psychosis, there is also a difference between the third and the ninth in which psychosis is more closely related to the third house of the practical intellect. On the other hand, neurotic tendencies relate more clearly to the ninth house of the higher mentality. House cusps in signs of the same rulers give a strong connection between sexuality and general outlook or philosophy; that is, over-inhibition and repression under certain circumstances.

Sublimation and transmutation are quite specific and can affect either heterosexual or homosexual inclinations—fifth or eleventh house—and appear as a displacement into work or the pursuit of status or the profession when the rulers of the fifth or the eleventh are in the tenth house or on the Midheaven. Or there may be a transposition onto a non-material super-mundane plane when these rulers are located in the eighth house; or a connection with the philosophy and Weltanschauung may take place when either the ruler of the fifth house or the eleventh is located in the ninth. Less negative in effect is when the ruler of the ninth house is located in the fifth or eleventh; this externalizes for the most part in a strong ethical streak.

This sublimation or displacement is shown for the heterosexual component through the location of the ruler of the fifth house in the tenth house and in the Midheaven as in Figures 4, 32, 33, as well as 8, 13, and 16; for the displacement of the homosexual component I gave no example, but a similar situation occurs when powerful and important planets are located near the cusp of the eleventh house yet still actually in the tenth. The tendency to non-materialization through location of the ruler of the fifth in the eighth is shown in Figure 10; the same for the homosexual component is seen by Figure 30, in the same way but retrograde in Figure 12, the same and in conjunction with the horoscope ruler is seen in Figure 17. A ninth house position for the ruler of the fifth house is shown by Figures 6 (also retrograde), 26, and 31; the same for the ruler of the eleventh house in Figure 33 and in Figure 8 (retrograde), while in Figures 8 and 30 the ruler of the eleventh house is at the same time the dispositor of the ruler of the fifth. As to the negative effect of the relationship to the ninth house, it should be pointed out that it is here a matter of negative effects which are not unqualified or absolute. For how is an era which takes its civilization to be culture to be able to distinguish individual ethos from universal morality? Thus is made clear the general negative effect when the ruler of the ninth is placed in the fifth or the eleventh.

I repeat that these days specific factors are required to cause homosexuality to become manifest. In general, it will be a minus in the direction of heterosexuality. But there are cases in which homosexuality is found with such absolute preponderance that the natives are quite indifferent to the opposite sex, yet there are no neurotic traits to be found. Even as profound a psychoanalytic thinker as W. Stekel considered this at least theoretically possible since all material taken from a physician's files is necessarily one-sided and always will be. In any case, one would expect to find in such a case the ruler of the eleventh house placed on the cusp of that house and with good aspects, while the ruler of the fifth would be found in the eighth.

But in general several forces are required to set homosexuality into motion, and the astrologer would these days do well to consider first the various specific indications of the constellation and to weigh these carefully one against the other before he comes to the diagnosis of overt homosexuality.

Most clear of all are the cases where the ruler of the eleventh house is located in the fifth, whether peregrine or in exile; that is, when the ruler of the fifth house is at the same time dispositor of the meanings and affairs of the eleventh house, or vice-versa when the ruler of the fifth is in the eleventh. In the first situation the aspirations connected with friendships operate at the same time in a heterosexual direction, as in Figures 10, 15, 19, and 20. In the latter case, as in Figures 4 and 6 where the ruler of the eleventh house is in exile in the fourth house, there occurs along with the orientation of the heterosexual inclinations some transformation in the area of friendships; in Figure 4, a sublimation into work as the ruler of the fifth is dispositor of the eleventh and in the Midheaven; in Figure 6 a neurotic inhibition as the ruler of the fifth is dispositor of the ruler of the eleventh and located in the ninth house; in Figure 20 a neurosis as the ruler of the fifth is dispositor of the ruler of the eleventh and located in the sixth house. The position of the ruler of the fifth house not in exile in the eleventh house is shown in Figure 9 where a sexual element is introduced strongly into the friendships; in Figure 27 where the Sun ruling the fifth is on the cusp of the eleventh house; in Figure 30 where the ruler of the fifth is in exile in the eleventh, and the ruler of the eleventh house is located at the cusp of the ninth—this further displacement being a certain indication of neurotic inhibitions. Finally, in Figures 8, 16, 23, 24, the ruler of the eleventh house is at the same time the dispositor of the ruler of the fifth house.

In these cases a preponderance of one component will occur; for example, a preponderance in the direction of friendships when the ruler of the eleventh house is strong and standing on its house cusp, and the ruler of the fifth house occupies a much less striking position, as in Figures 14, 24, 25, and 26.

To facilitate the understanding of these interpretations I want to introduce and examine here a case of heterosexuality (see Figure 34 on the following page).

Here we find Uranus in the fifth house trine the Ascendant, along with Venus, ruler of the eleventh house and conjunct Saturn ruling the seventh, while the ruler of the fifth house— Mars—is in exact conjunction with the ascendant. The result is a sexuality completely saturated with eros-a sexuality that will also be an expression of his eros. This is the case of an outwardly completely heterosexual man who has been attached for many years in a non-legal union with a woman who sometimes gives the impression of being a man dressed up in drag. On one occasion this couple went with a male friend into a gay night spot and when they were not dancing with each other, Konrad S. was asked to dance by the other men present, while the homosexual friend accompanying the couple was not. Konrad S. seemed to belong to the group while his friend did not. Of course it may depend on the times in which we live whether this man loves

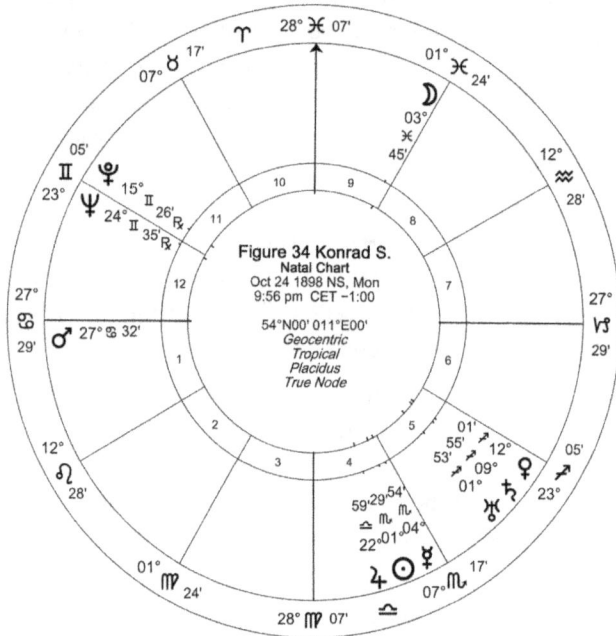

Figure 34 Konrad S.
Natal Chart
Oct 24 1898 NS, Mon
9:56 pm CET −1:00

54°N00' 011°E00'
Geocentric
Tropical
Placidus
True Node

the man in the woman or in sex is oriented towards the idea of a friend; the boundaries between heterosexuality and homosexuality are—and not only because of the behavior of the modern woman—by no means absolute.

These types can be grouped into those cases of homosexuality described in chapter 2 where the eleventh house is strongly tenanted while the fifth house has no planets. "Cases occur with a quite striking preponderance of homosexual factors which, however, are quite without any apparent loss of heterosexuality. . . ." (quoting directly from chapter 2).

These cases include those described above where the ruler of the eleventh house is in a good cosmic state on the cusp of that house (Figures 14, 24, 25, 26), or where the horoscope ruler is located in the eleventh house (Figures 4, 21—in this case moving to the cusp of the twelfth; 25, 27, 31—retrograde; and 32—dispositor of the horoscope ruler), or in which the ruler of the eleventh house stands in close relationship with the horoscope ruler, as in Figure 17 where the eleventh house ruler is retrograde and located in the eighth house in conjunction with it, or in Figure 22 where the eleventh house ruler is at the same time dispositor of the ruler of the fifth house and conjunct both the Ascendant and its ruler; also in Figures 23 and 29 where it is in conjunction solely with the Ascendant, or in Figure 28 where the ruler of the eleventh house is also the horoscope ruler. Included also are those cases where Uranus is in the eleventh house and has good aspects, or possibly also in the seventh, or is connected in some harmonious way with the Ascendant or the horoscope ruler (Figures 10, 11).

"Cases of men with a male eros penetrating their entire nature and resulting in an eros-type attractive power which is never sexualized, and where we can in no way find any indications of a mechanism of repression. . . ."

These are the cases in which the eleventh house factors are emphasized but are connected with the eighth house or the first house, as when for example the ruler of the eleventh is located in the eighth or the first, or Uranus is in the first house as in Figure 30, 31, 32; also when Neptune is well aspected in the eleventh house—a nevertheless troublesome position causing a blurring or disintegration of eleventh house affairs.

"Others show a chronic failure and misfortune in their love-life without any homosexual factors appearing to explain it. . . ."

These are cases in which, for example, the ruler of the fifth house is located in the twelfth as in Figure 7 or 25, or is in favorable state but located in the sixth house as in Figure 14, or, as already mentioned, Venus is in the twelfth house.

"Or even a kind of traumaphilia of their heterosexuality. . . ."

This is shown when the ruler of the fifth house is in a bad cosmic state or is retrograde or intercepted in the sixth house and in addition is badly aspected; in other words, planets which are unfavorable through their cosmic state or their location.

"Or, where some small but critical stimulus in the heterosexual life has been sufficient to lead the individual into homosexuality, without this basic component seeming to receive any particular emphasis. . . ."

This occurs when the ruler of the fifth house is in opposition to the Ascendant but located in the sixth or retrograde as in Figures 17, 18, 19, 20, 21. In particular this position of the ruler of the fifth house works as an obstacle which diverts a current; with any kind of suitable situation for the affairs of the eleventh house the sexuality will tend to orient itself in this direction.

"Or cases where the two basic components seem about equal in strength and the question must remain open why the homosexuality so completely suppressed the heterosexuality. . . ."

This is the result when the eleventh house is over-tenanted but not spoiled or vitiated and when the ruler of the fifth house is in the eleventh, or when by direction the ruler of the eleventh or Uranus forms aspects with the horoscope ruler or the Ascendant.

"Or those cases where homosexuality apparently sets the stage for an unexplained tendency to neurotic reactions, inhibitions, paranoid tendencies, and the use of drugs. . . ."

These are represented by those cases where the ruler of the eleventh house is placed in the sixth or the ninth or the twelfth houses (as in Figures 3, 5, 7, 8, 9, 22, 30, 31, 33) or where Neptune is retrograde in the eleventh house (Figures 10, 11) or intercepted there (Figure 8) or retrograde there as well as intercepted (Figure 6) or standing too close to the cusp of the twelfth (Figure 7, 9). Or where Uranus is retrograde in the fifth house (Figure 7) or intercepted there (Figures 3, 4, 5, 8) or retrograde there as well as intercepted (Figure 9), or near the cusp of the sixth or in the sixth (Figures 12, 13, 16). Or where the ruler of the eleventh house is strong and powerful but unfavorably aspected, or unfavorably aspects the horoscope ruler or the Ascendant.

This summary shows that in most of the cases shown here neurotic traits are to be found.

There is another interesting possibility in connection with the unfavorable planets located in the sixth or the twelfth. This is the case of the "queer-chaser"—the one who despises homosexuals and was called by Bluher a "persecuting type." The theory goes that this person does battle with inner difficulties by selecting other individuals in whom he perceives the same problem and reacting inappropriately and exaggeratedly, and the astrological indication of this is where Uranus or the ruler of the eleventh house is located in the sixth house. On the other hand, those who have Uranus or the ruler of the eleventh house located in the twelfth house are more paranoid and more inhibited but are rather inexpressive about their conscious feelings of inferiority, and do not show the aggression and lack of logic or self-insight that characterizes those with Uranus in the sixth.

I will not go into an examination here of the significance of the fourth and third houses to the extent that I have already done for the fifth and the eleventh. These houses may show the difficulties already mentioned where the sexual drive becomes attached in some way to a parent or a brother or sister. Also, I have already emphasized that in autoerotic cases there is an increased significance of the horoscope ruler or of the first house itself. Nor is it necessary to go further into the astrological basis for the Jungian division of personalities into extroverted or introverted types whereby extroversion is conceived of meaning that one's actions are externally or object-oriented, other than to relate extroversion to either the houses above the horizon and introversion to the houses beneath, or to the houses in the western half of the horoscope and introversion to the houses in the eastern half.

I see no reason to go further into the aspects in general. This would be without purpose since the aspects are dynamic mechanisms depending entirely on the essential nature and the determinations of the planets involved in them. Nothing is worse than a schematic classification of aspects, which from time to time is undertaken by astrological "statisticians," without taking into consideration the planets' determinations; the "results" are always nonsense.

Perhaps it would be possible to bring graphology into the picture as a help to astrology. The means and methods are quite different but any one way of arriving at valid goals should not preclude the value of another and different way. Also, F. Werle, in a work which has not yet been published, has used a different method and has come to some interesting conclusions. His method proceeds from the theory that the horoscope expresses three fundamental illnesses and that these are determined by the position of the Sun, Moon, and ascendant alone. In this method there are similarities to one used by Paracelsus.

I want to emphasize that the study of the character-constellation must always be synthetic and that here, just as in psychoanalysis, an analysis of individual details without consideration of the whole and its interdependent parts is purposeless, unfruitful, mechanistic, and unable to produce valid conclusions.

Chapter 7

FEMALE HOMOSEXUALITY

Even before my analytical experience proved the truth of it to me, I had always been of the opinion that there was a complete difference between male and female homosexuality.

That male homosexuality gains its great significance through the male. eros was gone into in earlier chapters. But there is no female eros, and from this fact alone an attempt to equate male and female homosexuality would be false. In any case, the precise meaning and extent of this eros is still not perceived, in part because it does not concur with accepted dogmas and because certain emotional attitudes prevent it, or because it simply goes beyond the conceptualization of many people.

I am of the opinion that there must be, corresponding to the eros factor among men, which is separate from the factor of heterosexuality, a similar factor among women which is likewise distinct from their heterosexuality. This is the factor of motherhood. Female homosexuality originates almost always from deviations of this mother-child complex, and secondly from their heterosexuality. Virile characteristics play in active lesbianism a much greater role than among the more passive representatives of this so-called "homosexuality." Freud himself observed the high degree of independence between psychic and physical hermaphroditism but added the reservation that "this independence is more clear for men than for women, where the physical and mental expressions of the opposite sexual character combine together rather according to rule." This means that with female homosexuality one will usually discover a physical type with masculine features, which Kretschmer assigned to the dysplastics. The relationship between the masculine type of woman to schizothymia is beyond doubt as well as its similarity to the leptosomic physical type. From the conclusions drawn in chapter 3 it can be understood that strong male characteristics can—but do not have to—indicate a homosexual orientation.

Also, the meaning of the fifth-eleventh house opposition is consequently altered. For the man it is love (fifth) and friendship (eleventh), sex (fifth) and eros (eleventh); for the woman it is sexuality and children (fifth), eroticism and flirtation (eleventh). Also, among women creative works are much more evident from the tenth and eleventh houses than from the fifth house. In astrology, womanliness shows its sex-based character—more clearly seen with women than with men—where Venus and the Moon are in earth or water signs; Mercury can be included. This is shown in the menstruation cycle.

There exists a stronger relationship between woman and the water and earth signs, as I have already pointed out in the chapter on constitution. For this reason water and earth signs on the cusp of the fifth house are for women more fruitful, while it is the other way around for men for whom fire and air signs on this cusp are more fruitful. So apart from the planets and aspects involved, the position of fire or air signs on the cusps of the fifth and eleventh houses has considerable significance. A preponderance of male factors—whether through the important positions of masculine planets or through a masculine sign rising—should always be given our attention because it is never lacking in cases of active lesbianism. For the more passive types Neptune in the seventh house is the strongest and most significant factor.

Female Homosexuality

In cases among men with favorable Uranus in the eleventh or fifth house, the aspects and determinations enable one to recognize in the native a worthwhile and productive eros type; the same arrangement works catastrophically for women! Oscar Schmitz has said about Uranus: "Only he who is highly evolved will experience Uranus's influence as other than disrupting," and this is true because eros is rooted both in and beyond homosexuality—but true only for men. The effects of Uranus and Neptune exchange places for men and for women. Not the masculine Uranus, but rather the feminine Neptune is the general significator of female homosexuality.

It is unnecessary to demonstrate this here by introducing more examples. More important in considering female homosexuality is the fact that disharmonious aspects of Venus more frequently bring forth disharmonious results. Female homosexuality always has something of chaos and illusion about it in contrast to the intuition of the Uranian eros. So, from the standpoint of general psychology it must be said that with respect to Uranus and Neptune female homosexuality bears a much closer relationship to Neptune.

Guido Bonatus says that in female horoscopes Venus and Mars in connection with Saturn in the eastern half of the horoscope and in masculine signs make male lovers of no interest to the native, while in feminine signs and in the western half the situation is reversed. I can support this. Generally women are more secretive, withdrawn, and reserved in their homosexuality than are men. Frigidity is common. A strong indication of the truth of my psychoanalytical hypothesis was the exceptional significance of the fourth house for the native's mother, and to some extent the third house; as important factors these houses far outweighed the ninth or the eleventh. In my opinion female homosexuality is proven to be based on either a constitutional factor or a neurotic one which is specifically connected with the mother.

Chapter 8

HETEROPHILIA
AND HOMOPHILIA

In 1924 in a monograph which had the same title as this chapter and was published by the Academic Study Group of Berlin (now the Midgard Publishing House) I examined the forces of attraction working among men. On this subject I will now give briefly my astrological conclusions since they are likely to make more clear the nature of "sympathy" between individuals as well as unaccountable attraction in love.

When we observe a sudden passionate love which is extremely strong, in which the native is unable to see the real value or actual nature of the object, we then shall most likely find in analysis that within the native strong factors of repetition are at work; it is not the object per se which is loved but an object which is at least in part an illusion, a mosaic of earlier subjective-objective experiences which in the last analysis go back to the very earliest impressions of childhood (Oedipus complex).

And yet one also sees that very frequently, perhaps just in those cases of the strongest "fatal attraction" and even "at first sight" these factors are not sufficient to explain the situation. Since sometimes almost none of the abovementioned factors can be found a satisfying analysis is impossible if other different factors are not allowed.

In any case, this "sympathy" between individuals can be observed and formulated by astrological methods; we usually find in cases of strong and unusual attraction that there is an extensive relationship between the planetary positions of both persons—in the sense of complementation or heterophilia, or of similarity or homophilia.

This brings us to the extensive area of comparative horoscopy, so that I can only make here a few observations concerning principles and general significance.

The relationship between the planetary positions can be such that, for example, Mars and Venus of both horoscopes are connected to each other by aspect or perhaps through Mars occupying the same degree of the male nativity that Venus occupies in the female—a conjunction as it were. Or these planetary relationships are in mutual aspect in some way. Of course strong connections by aspect will be found as a bond in both a sympathetic and inimical sense, wherein we have a restatement of that basic analytical rule concerning ambivalence—that love is not the opposite of hate but of indifference.

Quite specific, more or less one-sided character traits appear in relationship with one another depending on the planets which have the closest contact with each other. That the many love relationships of a person show similar, individualistic features only makes this observation even more constructive from the point of view of astrology and psychology.

I should like to add that Sun positions in opposition or square by no means result in antipathy, but instead a quite possibly adequate complementation. For example, I have in my files a person who is a strong Gemini type with his Ascendant at 8o Gemini and the Sun conjunct Mercury and Jupiter in Gemini while Mars in Gemini is on the cusp of the second house; this person met a predominantly Sagittarius type who fell hopelessly in love with him. The Gemini person had his Descendant on the other's Uranus exact to ten minutes, Jupiter on the cusp of his fifth house (the other had Jupiter conjunct and parallel the Sun which was ruler of the fifth house; Aquarius was on the eleventh) and Uranus on the cusp of the twelfth house, his Sun and Mercury opposed to Mercury and the Sun of the other, his Mars opposite Saturn of the other (Saturn was in the eleventh in both horoscopes) and Mars conjunct the other's Neptune and within orb of an opposition to Venus and the Moon of the other (both had the Moon in Capricorn); his Moon was in the twelfth house of the other but well aspected.

I have also found cases where the same planets occupy the same zodiacal degree or where predominantly the same planets occupy the same houses; these are connections that are not so close, but for certain kinds of persons seem to provide an extraordinary power of attraction.

This difference was particularly striking for me since at the time I published my monograph on attraction I had not evaluated my material from the viewpoint of astrology.

I had brought out in that article that the relation between male and female components of psychic structure found interplay not only between man and woman as a connection between different poles—heterophilia—but that to this "normal" relation between male and female there corresponded "perverted" ones such as that of the so-called virile homosexual to the more feminine passive homosexual (as in ancient literature) or of the more effeminate man to a masculine woman. So, while these connections are effects which follow the rules of the bipolar tendency to complementation—to heterophilia—the other principle of attraction is clearly monopolar—toward homophilia. Homophilia is also the principle of attraction involved in friendship, in eras, and in the companionate marriage. Of course both powers of attraction occur in some kind of a mixture. Heterophilic elements can transform a homophilic love of friends into love towards young men, for in general the possibility of perversion always exists, and just in the same sense that the principles of object choice—with no alteration of the quality or composition of the forces of attraction-are in operation in the choice of object among the opposite sex. There are those cases in which someone loves the man in the woman (perverted homophilia) or the young girl in the young man (perverted heterophilia). For examples we have Achilles and Patroclus along with Achilles and Penthesilea, and also Siegfried and Brunhilde (homophilia) in contrast with Siegfried and Krimhilde (heterophilia).

It would be superfluous to give a long list of examples here and the material is not easy to come by. There is very little material in the area of contemporary athletics and also very little from marriages either in history or in the present time with a close connectedness indicated also by a mutual aspect. For example, an unfavorable Saturn in a man's horoscope on top of Venus or the Moon in a woman's horoscope; in the very best of situations this would result in a "lord-and-master" kind of marriage which is not the kind envisioned by the church or by society.

Judgment as to whether a mutual planetary connectedness is complementary (heterophilic) or similar (homophilic) is of course necessary and does not have to be explained here any further; I have already pointed out that these laws of attraction represent extremes.

Let us consider another example—that of Hans A., Figure 24. The native experienced an affair that began suddenly and violently when his Ascendant progressed to the sextile of Venus, his eleventh house ruler. His Sun at 0° Virgo was conjunct the Moon of his friend at 5° Virgo; his Moon at 24° Sagittarius was conjunct the Sun of the other at 25° Sagittarius; his Jupiter at 3° Capricorn was conjunct the other's Uranus at 3° Capricorn, while his own Uranus at 12° Sagittarius was conjunct the other's Venus at 12° Sagittarius. Less harmonious were connections such as the native's Mercury at 27° Leo at the Midheaven opposed to the other's Saturn at 28° Aquarius in the sixth house; his own eighth house Neptune at 1° Cancer was opposed to his friend's Uranus at 3° Capricorn; and his own retrograde Saturn at 10° Capricorn was opposed to the retrograde Neptune of the other at 9° Cancer.

In my opinion this is a most extraordinary example of connection through aspect; I have never seen an example where the indications are so close. However, most material shows planetary relationships which are similar.

I have also observed that between patient and analyst there is frequently the same kind of mutual aspects that we have been examining. Reactions in this area are typical and unmistakable; I do not mean with respect to the transference itself as much as in the characteristic forms the patient's transference takes. In analysis transference takes place in the sense that the analyst enters into the role of the most important figure at the time of the formation of the neurosis, be it with respect to the mother, the father, or the sister, or whomever -all of which can be observed from the patient's dreams.

And yet I believe that close mutual aspects between analyst and patient are also of great importance here. I recall the case of a forty-five year old patient with whom I played the role of an "older man" despite the fact that at that time I was only twenty-five years old. In this case the closest aspect was the fact that my Saturn, which was stronger both in its cosmic state and its accidental position, was placed right on his Mars. At the time I had wondered about this relationship and finally concluded there was some kind of father-son complex at work between us, possibly conditioned by some factor connected with the patient's fantasy of having an older brother (he was actually an only child), but I was nagged by the feeling that this explanation was inadequate.

I also take considerable interest in why a patient entertains in his dreams fantasies of murder towards his analyst which go far beyond what the psychoanalytical situation would seem to imply. In one such case out of my practice I found that the closest mutual aspect was a square between my Mars and the patient's Mars, which in his particular case was central to the reason for his neurosis.

Chapter 9

PRINCE OF WALES AND HIS PARENTS

This connectedness is quite naturally most clearly seen in the horoscopes of people who are in fact related by blood, and on the basis of my knowledge I am completely of the opinion that the problem of heredity is fully explainable as long as astrological factors are included in the analysis.

It is generally understood that there is a difference between the genotype—the type as it lies, so to speak, in the absolute totality of hereditary factors—and the actual phenotype. Tracing the phenotype in earlier generations was work that led to satisfying and noteworthy observations; the work of Robert Sommer is particularly to be noted. However, after giving consideration to the data from botany and zoology it was possible to state specific laws. The entire subject of the study of heredity is founded on the work of Mendel, who was at one time completely unknown but who first pointed the way to a systematic knowledge in this area. Also the work of Kretschmer should be mentioned in connection with his observation of families: "Neither the physical constitution nor the psychological make-up are constitution in the strictest sense, that is, inherited traits. Both of them, as well as personality, are only portions of the phenotypic manifestation of the collective factors of inheritance." Impure or mixed types are always products of hereditary factors in ascendancy which differ or deviate from each other. This mixture must be analyzed backwards in the family to understand its origins.

The study of heredity must of course go beyond strictly family factors; they must include an understanding of race. Kretschmer's types are present in all racial types, it has been said, and we are inclined to agree with this from astro-typological considerations. A certain affinity between the leptosomic physique, schizothymia and the nordic race already has been pointed out by certain authors, with the consequence that the Aquarius type can more easily and more strongly make its appearance within such a racial mass of hereditary factors; it can appear in a more pure type as similarly the asthenic type can without pyknics among its forefathers. For this reason we have already quoted Selva on how astrological influences are in dependence on the given material, as it were, and this particularly so in heredity. And it is only astrology that provides the means of discovering how the totality of heredity factors from the parents and grandparents—from both sides of one's family—leads to the specific mixture in the resulting children; for the important question is the way in which these factors are developed.

An attempt to show the actual mechanics of inheritance in some accordance with laws, that is to show which of the parents or grandparents can and must be the one whose heredity will predominate, was done by H. Swoboda, particularly in his work "The Year of Seven" in vol. 1 of his *Heredity*. With considerable data at his disposal Swoboda showed that the Descendants receive the hereditary factors most strongly when the individuals are in age in some multiple of their ancestor's seventh year, that is, 28, 35, 42, 49, etc., Or, an individual resembles in greater ways that one of his forefathers whose birth year is distant to his own by a multiple of seven.

By way of example we had Figure 3 of F. H., and we stated

that the brother of the native took after his father while F. H. did not. When the brother was born the father was twenty-eight years and three months old; however, no such multiple of seven existed at the time F. H. was born. Swoboda also considered homosexuality in some depth in this regard. Figure 4, Frederick the Great, born January 24, 1712, had a brother, Prince Heinrich, born January 18, 1726, who was also homosexual; the difference between the two in age is two times seven years. In their ancestors the seven-year cycle appeared on the side of the mother's parents—the house of Orange—who go back in turn to King James I of England, born June 16, 1566, and who was homosexual. Homosexuality appeared frequently among his Descendants. His son Charles I of England (1625-1649) had a daughter Mary who married the ruler William II of Orange, whose son was William III of Orange, King of England (1689-1702) born November 14, 1650, and who was homosexual. Also homosexual was his cousin and heir Queen Anne (1702-1714) who was born on February 6, 1665, and who was the daughter of King James II (1685-1688). The distance of the birth year of James I of England to William III of Orange is twelve times seven years; William III of Orange to Anne of England is two times seven years.

Another cousin and granddaughter of Charles I was the wife of Phillip of Orleans, Henriette. Their granddaughter, the Princess of Savoy, Marie Adelaide, born December 1685, was also homosexual. The distance from Queen Anne to her niece twice removed was three times seven years. And again from the latter to the Hohenzollern Frederick the Great there was four times seven years. Likewise, James I's older sister Elizabeth, the consort of the German King of the Palitinate, had a daughter Sophie, born October 1630, who married Ernst August, the first elector of Hanover. Their daughter Sophie Charlotte, born October 20, 1668, married Frederick I of Prussia. Her son, Frederick William I married his cousin Sophie Dorothea, daughter from the first marriage of George I, King of Great Britain and Ireland (1714-

1727), who was born on March 28, 1660; the latter's first wife had been Sophie Dorothea of Luneberg, and he was, of course, the successor of Queen Anne.

From the marriage of Frederick William I there were, among others, as said, Frederick the Great, Ulrica, Prince Heinrich, Prince August William. The brother-in-law of Frederick William I was George II of England, born October 30, 1683; his grandson and successor King George III, born June 4, 1738, was homosexual as was also the latter's brother Earnest August of Cumberland (1771-1857). Swoboda calculated the seven-year cycle from Frederick the Great and his brother Heinrich to Marie Adelaide of Savoy as four times seven and six times seven, respectively; also from Frederick the Great through his brother August William to the homosexual King Ludwig of Bavaria he found twelve times seven years. Moreover, from Frederick the Great to the present Prince of Wales there is twenty-six times seven years. In fact, the cycle passes neither onto George II of England—the grandfather of Queen Victoria—nor his brother, nor to his nephew the homosexual Gustav II of Sweden, son of Frederick the Great's sister, Ulrica. But the regularity of the cycle is nevertheless striking.

In addition, among the Swedes one thinks of the masculine Queen Christina, who had Hohenzollern blood, and of Charles XII of Sweden, also presumed to be homosexual. Swoboda also describes King Louis XIII of France and his brother Gaston of Orleans as homosexual and claims that the latter's son Philippe II and his daughters Louise Adelaide and Louise Elisabeth were all homosexual; Swoboda shows these are all related by the seven-year cycle.

It is difficult to avoid the concept that homosexuality is also a hereditary trait—for the most part latent and recessive—but appearing frequently when the strains are crossed in a significant way. Von Romer cites a family wherein it appears as high as thirty-five percent. But of course in families where marriage occurs among relatives the latent or recessive factors will be thrown up much more often and more easily, which perhaps explains why among the European dynasties and aristocracy it appears with quite high frequency. Freud himself had observed this peculiarity but felt that it was to be explained in terms of an infantile fixation on the ever-present male servants. However, when one considers the problem of eras and its significance in the concept of leadership, it seems possible that the origin of a class of nobility must be "erocratic," that is, such individuals must carry a stronger homosexual component among them than would be found among the common folk.

A similar concept arises in this matter from a study of Kretschmer's types. The leptosomes, perhaps because of their increased homosexuality, set themselves up as rulers and develop an exclusive caste system of aristocratic natures. One thinks of the tall, noble caste among the Indians. The tall, aristocratic class "that is found throughout the entire world," is mainly a leptosomicschizothymic type, or from the point of view of astrology, an Aquarius-Sagittarius type.

The student of heredity must get hold of a system with which he can recognize how the recessive factors again return to dominance; astrology gives this.

The works by Paul Flambart on this subject have not been given sufficient consideration—presumably because they are too good and too inaccessible. I am speaking here of *La Portee de l'Astrologie Scientifique* (1914), and *Memoire sur l'Astrologie Scientifique* given at the Third International Congress for Experimental Psychology in Paris, 1913, and of two smaller works *Etude Nouvelle sur l'Heredite* (1903), and *La Loi d'Heredite Astrale* (1919). It was Flambart who introduced the concept of statistical method into astrology, but without any nonsensical statistical schematism, and who summed up his observations on the matter in the following words: "The birth of a child takes place when the heavens—that is the horoscope for the moment of the first breath—have the strongest possible resemblance to the heavens of his forefathers." He notes in particular how in premature births of eight and even seven month pregnancies the actual birth time showed this resemblance in a much better way than could be so if the pregnancy had gone to its expected date of maturity. I can agree with this although my data on this subject include only several dozen horoscopes, since when I was working in a university obstetric clinic the problem of suicide and astrology was at that time of greater interest to me and so my attention was elsewhere. But it is also interesting to note that these factors also affect the ability for labor to take place. To return to the pair of twins A. H. and K. H. in chapter 2, it should be noted that for K. H. there was a period of from 1:00 to 2:15—the time that the sign Taurus took to rise—that birth was impossible. It struck me at the time that the difference of two hours between births from a single placenta was unusual. Therefore, a "corresponding" sign had to arrive on the Ascendant. A different sign always produces modifications (the physical differences between Aries A. H. and Gemini K. H.) but there is certainly an effect of a play of forces which must come together on a common denominator or many minutes must go by until the first breath is taken.

In order to give an example of how astrology can be shown in actual fact to be significant for heredity I have selected the horoscopes of the present Prince of Wales and his parents, because several points were not made clear during the examination of his horoscope earlier in chapter 5. I have taken the nativities from the English publication *Old Moore 's Messenger*.

In the horoscope of the monarchs the following similarities are at once striking:

King George V	Queen Mary
Neptune 10° Aries	Neptune 14° Aries
Venus 9° Taurus	Venus 3° Taurus
Mercury 18° Taurus	Mercury 29° Taurus
Mars 5° Leo	Mars 15° Leo

00° ♑ 46'

19° ♑ 02'

12° ♐ 39'

♃ 25° ♐ 40' ℞

31' ♒ 13°

18° ♏ 48'

10

9

11

8

12

George V
Natal Chart
Jun 3 1865 NS, Sat
1:18 am UT +0:00
London, England
51°N30' 000°W10'
Geocentric
Tropical
Placidus
True Node

7

℞ 03' ♎ 24° ♄

02°
♈
01'

02°
♎
01'

♅ 10° ♈ 08'

03' ♎ 01° ☽

1

6

♀ 09° ♉ 38'
☿ 13° ♉ 24'
18° ♉ 28'

♍

18° ♉ 48'

2

5

3

4

35' ♌ 05°
♂

31' ♌ 13°

25' ♊
12°

34' ♊ 28'

12° ♊ 39'

☉

♅

19° ♋ 02'

00° ♋ 46'

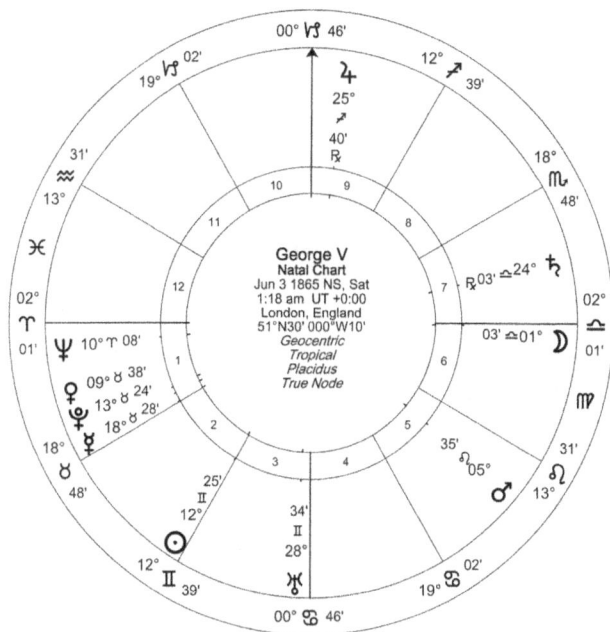

In both horoscopes the signs Capricorn and Virgo are untenanted.

Let us compare the nativity of the Prince of Wales with those of his parents. His Ascendant, which has the opposition to Mercury, sextile of Mars, semi-sextile of the Moon, quincunx of the Sun, and a wide square to Uranus, is located at 3° Aquarius and is conjunct the Ascendant of his mother at 6° Aquarius and stands also conjunct with his grandmother Queen Alexandra's Saturn at 3° Aquarius (Saturn is his horoscope ruler). His Moon is semisextile the Ascendant as it is also in the horoscope of his mother; his father has the Moon in opposition to his own Ascendant. His first house Moon at 3° Pisces is conjunct the Moon of his mother at 8° Pisces—the sign is intercepted in the first house in both horoscopes and it is conjunct his mother's Jupiter at 6° Pisces. His Mars at 0° Aries is conjunct his father's Ascendant at 2° Aries and has a trine to the father's Mars located at 5° Leo.

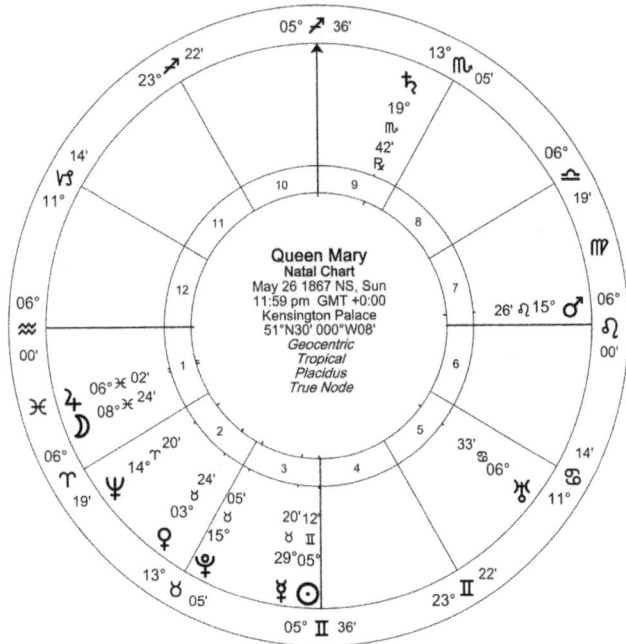

Queen Mary
Natal Chart
May 26 1867 NS, Sun
11:59 pm GMT +0:00
Kensington Palace
51°N30' 000°W08'
Geocentric
Tropical
Placidus
True Node

His third house Venus is in Taurus as it is in the horoscopes of both his parents; at 23° Taurus it is sextile Mercury; it is conjunct the Taurus Mercury of his father at 18° and the Mercury of his mother at 29° and perhaps it is noteworthy that the cusp of his own fourth house is close to this degree.

His IC at 3° Gemini takes the square of the Moon, as it does in the horoscopes of his mother and father; it is conjunct the IC of his mother at 5° Gemini and is sextile to the Neptune of his father and mother and conjunct the father's Sun at 12° Gemini. His Jupiter at 18° Gemini has only a wide connection by opposition with the Jupiter of his father, retrograde at 25° Sagittarius (the father has Jupiter opposed to Uranus), but there is a close opposition with the Jupiter of his grandfather King Edward VII who had the planet at 21° Sagittarius (and who had Jupiter square Uranus).

The Sun of the prince is in the fifth at 2° Cancer and has a conjunction with the IC of his father at 0° Cancer and has a conjunction with the fifth house Uranus of his mother at 6° Cancer.

Mercury at 27° Cancer in the sixth house has a sextile to his mother's Mercury, and in the father's horoscope the untenanted sign Virgo is intercepted in the sixth house. Remember that this Mercury, which is in a wide opposition to the Ascendant, seemed significant as the ruler of the prince's fifth house.

The prince's Descendant at 3° Leo is conjunct his father's Mars at 5° Leo, while his own Mars is conjunct his father's Ascendant at 2° Aries.

The Prince has 3° Libra on the cusp of his eighth house and this lies on the Descendant of his father—does this indicate the succession to the father's throne upon the latter's death?—and this degree is conjunct the father's Moon at 1o Libra, which in turn is conjunct the Moon of King Edward VII at 2° Virgo.

Saturn at 18° Libra has a wide conjunction with the father's Saturn at 24° Libra and a semisextile with the mother's Saturn at 19° Scorpio.

In these examples it is noteworthy that there is really no planet that does not have some similar or mutual relationship to some element in the horoscopes of his parents and his grandparents. I must emphasize that these relationships do not occur with 100 percent regularity in comparison with the horoscopes of the parents alone, but demonstrate some relationship to the horoscopes of the grandparents as well.

Flambart prepared himself against the objection that it was a matter of coincidence by calculating the normal statistical frequencies. The murdered Czar Nicholas II had the Moon conjunction Jupiter, which occurs in the horoscopes of both his parents, and in the same sign as his mother's; like his mother it receives the square of Venus and Uranus. The chances for the conjunction are 1:5832; that of the square 1:81. The conjunction of the Sun and Saturn has a percentage average of seven percent, yet in the horoscopes of the seven children of Emperor William II (Kaiser Wilhelm) it occurs three times—in the horoscopes of the crown prince, Prince Oscar, and Princess Victoria Luisa. The emperor had the Sun opposition Saturn. The square of Mars to Venus in the emperor's horoscope is also found in the horoscope of Prince Joachim, the sextile in the horoscopes of the crown prince and Prince Adalbert, the conjunction in that of Prince August Wilhelm, the semisextile in that of Prince Eitel Friedrich, and the quincunx in the horoscope of the princess. The Ascendant of the crown prince is 8o Sagittarius and that is the same degree as the Ascendant of his own son Prince Louis Ferdinand. It seems plain enough that these astrological factors are to be attributed to the ones appearing in the father's horoscope.

Astrology sheds light on the interesting fact that birthdates within a family sometimes occur in the same degree, which fact goes quite beyond the studies of periodicity done by W. Fliess and H. Swoboda. Once again the case of Frederick the Great is instructive: His birthdate was January 24, 1712, his nephew King Gustav III of Sweden January 24, 1757, his sister Sophie Dorothea January 25, 1 719, and only a few days earlier his brother Henrich on January 18, 1726. His sister Ulrica, mother of the homosexual Gustav III, was born July 24, 1720—showing the appearance of the point of opposition to the Sun's position.

The prospects for a science of heredity assisted by the study of astrology are really considerable. Perhaps it is also possible that there may be racial traits that relate to astrological factors since, after all, races are only large, extended families. In this case the relationships would be similar to those in mundane astrology.

Chapter 10

THE USE OF
PSYCHOANALYSIS

M y purpose is twofold—one is practical and is concerned
with psychoanalysis, while the other is theoretical and relates to the possibility of making astrology useful in the development of a more objective science of the psyche; it is this latter
purpose which is more important to me, for there are no better
methods for an understanding of character. The picture that is
finally put together through long analysis of the so-called orga-
nizational form means very little in reality. Claims such as the
following of Freud, for example, are really quite hypothetical:
"An emphasis on anal eroticism at the pregenital stage will leave
behind in a man a significant predisposition to homosexuality
when the next step of the sexual function—that of the primacy
of the genitalia-is reached'; (from his "Disposition to Obsses-
sional Neurosis," *Collected Works*, vol. 5). And I am reluctant to
give any support to it.

We are certainly far away from any kind of study of medicine
based on astrology, nor are we dealing with that subject here,
but there are areas which cannot yet be comprehended by any
known technical methods of study and one of these areas is the
nature of the psyche. All methods of character analysis, which

in my opinion are far too little individualistic and insufficiently psychoanalytical, must now be tested for their synthetic value.

At a convention in Berlin on the subject "Constitution and Character," a certain Professor Dr. A.B. concluded his lecture with the words:

> In the final analysis, all methods which are being used in the research into our lives are incomplete and in need of fulfilling elements, and none will—cut off from the others—be able to reach its goal. The beginning and end of character-study is empathy for the individual, but this empathy is far from being a science. Will we succeed in grasping the nature of a human being—ill or well—with all his contrasts and contradictions in any final sense?

In reply, we can only wonder how many asking the question know anything about serious astrology.

I do not wish to go into the question of fate versus free-will except to say that psychoanalysis and so-called individual psychology (there is scarcely anything that could be less individualistic) must eventually discover that fate is individual—it is egocentric, and we must attempt to unmask those unknown forces of which Goethe says in his Egmont: "Man thinks he leads his life, leads himself, while his innermost being is irresistibly drawn towards his destiny." In any case, the materialistic tendencies in the study of character are both overextended and outdated, and I was brought to the conclusion that there must be introduced-parallel to the concept of the *constitution*—something similar for the psychological landscape—the *character-constellation*.

That there is a decided lack in psychoanalysis has been clearly expressed in the following remarks of H. Hartmann in his *Principles of Psychoanalysis*:

> Psychoanalysis attempts to establish a so-called "natural" system of character traits-somewhat analo-

gous to biological classifications based on the level of historical evolutionary development. But as long as we know little about the plausibility of the interaction of these character-forming factors—the sex drive, the dependence according to certain laws of the component or partial instincts and the erogenous zones on each other—and know little about the interaction of character traits in blocking or enhancing each other's development, this analytical attempt to explain the development of character must remain unfinished. Psychoanalysis can only furnish contributions to an etiology of character and must await fulfillment through further descriptive works and studies of psychological types. It was able, however, to reveal points of view and give partial explanations which for the general study of character have had a significance that should not be underestimated.

I agree with this statement word for word, and I also wish to give Hartmann's remarks in which he discusses the problem of the constitution:

It is the particular nature of the analytical method that accidental factors are more easily accessible to. it arid the study of constitutional factors must therefore remain in the background. Freud said: "The dispositional factor appears only after the accidental factor, as something that is perceived through experience." In the study of the organic and biological bases of development psychoanalysis can, despite its recognition of the somatic factors, contribute something as pure psychological discipline only in an indirect manner. But it should not be said that the effects of the constitutional factor would be overlooked or their significance not recognized. The constitutional strengthening of the erogenous zones in the analytical theory of both perversions and neuroses plays the decisive role and according to analysis furnished significant contributions to the formation of character in the normal individual.

I want to emphasize here that I consider this part of orthodox psychoanalytical teaching as hypothetical and even quite doubtful. Freudian theory proceeds on the premise that the sexual drive is formed out of the component or partial instincts corresponding to the erogenous zones—the mouth, anus, and genitals; that there is an oral, then an anal, and then a narcissistic stage before the primacy of the genital stage is reached, to which the other component instincts subordinate themselves. However, it cannot be told from the horoscope how a sadistic tendency will externalize—whether through beatings, stabbings, mental torments or whatever—but one *could* assess the quality and relative quantity of a sadistic constellation found in the horoscope. One can tell from the horoscope whether a man is avaricious or not but not whether he is anally erotic or not. I simply cannot believe in either the oral or the anal theory. I would not argue with the possibility of determining by analysis the importance of certain zones, but these are already secondary, are already "symbols" or expressions and manifestations of particular constellation factors in the personality.

And further: "Similarly, the expression of the oedipus complex in the individual is according to Freud determined by the relative degree of the constitutional bisexuality; again a factor of the greatest significance for the development of the personality in both the well or the sick individual." (F. Bohm thought there is a reverse oedipus complex comprised of a father fixation and hatred of the mother.)

I find myself in direct contradiction to these viewpoints. It is significant that Ferenczi suggested the word amphisexuality to be used with reference to the personality in contrast to the physiological term bisexuality. As always my point of view is that there are two basic components which among men are directed to the opposite sex and at the same time to the same sex, so that in my estimation the theory of the oedipus complex is much over-worked when it is not used solely as a diagnostic term but instead as the fundamental explanation of a certain development. Furthermore, the material that I have introduced along with the rationale of thought behind it shows clearly that the quotation of Freud given above must be essentially false.

Also false is the idea—widely accepted in psychoanalysis—that both the basic components are quantitatively similar in nature. One of the most basic mistakes of psychoanalysis is that it does not understand how to distinguish between sex and eros, and that sex is extended or broadened to become libido. According to orthodox psychoanalysis libido is always only sex; but libido is also made use of in the realm of the "platonic eros" and is even quite a part of it. In reality one finds sex, libido, and eros together.

I reject the sexual theory which postulates the hypothetical constitution of the zones and assumes that they are specific determining factors in the development of the personality. There then results a sharper and more practical basis for analysis—character organization according to the constellation. So too the modified psychoanalysis of Stekel has posed problems similar to those that Hartmann mentions, in the following:

> Another question whose answer could be of the greatest significance for the analytical ontogenesis of the sexual drive is the question of the degree of the specificity of its constitutional elements—the question of whether we are able to assume an independent sexual "component constitution," or whether more general dispositions also condition the development of the sex drive. Here also arises the further question concerning the necessary dependence or possible independence of certain ways of sexual behavior differing from the more general patterns of behavior. Moreover, for the development of analytical sexual theory it would be of great

value to have more certain knowledge as to whether the separate dispositions correspond to the separate structures of sexuality; whether this assumed independence from each other of the separate components has any reference to the relative power of the erogenous zones and the component instincts, and which among them; and finally, which features of the sex drive have some relation to each other through biological inheritance. But all these problems, whose solution, support, or correction would greatly serve analytical studies, are recognized even today as possible and even necessary questions; their development, however, has not progressed so far that an essential advance for analytical sexual theory can be anticipated through a loan from the hypotheses of biological inheritance.

Similar reflections had long occupied my mind, and the result has been this introduction of the theory of the *constellation*.

Is there any chance that this theory will be recognized as a valid answer to some of the above questions; will those who take their attitude for scientific be able to accept what astrology offers?

Astrology is a science and perhaps the most objective, or to put it better, the most objective for psychology, and if I take the trouble to attempt to make the results of astrology useful for psychoanalysis it is because my intention is to shorten the time that therapy takes, so that when the situation of transference has taken place the treatment can move forward systematically.

In the case of F. H., I presented an analysis based on astrology and concluded with a prediction which I can imagine may very well actually take place. So the question might arise as to why engage in lengthy analysis and therapy when what is going to happen must happen anyway. But who knows to what extent we are tools? Stekel once wrote: "The problem for the doctor is in the case of a neurotic to find the first sign of an incipient will to become well and to make a transformation in the will to illness."

Fatalism, particularly in a medical context, would be a senseless attitude. And I personally lay great store on knowing whether or for how long I must swim with or against the current, or whether the particular time of the actual therapeutic work is favorable or unfavorable. One can then protect himself from serious mistakes or unpleasant surprises of a psychiatric nature -or even unpreventable suicides. One can in effect exclude the incurable.

There is always the question then of whether we have any objective "measurable" standards for the psychological landscape. And precisely because the question exists there is such enthusiasm for the "measurable" types of Kretschmer, which have some connection with personality traits. P. Flambart once made the statement that the horoscope is the scientific formulation of the psyche, just because it is the sole objective one. Why then is more use not made of it? Is it because the passion for perceiving causality cannot be satisfied? Does the fact that the science of electricity really knows not at all what electricity is prevent the laws governing its action from being put to practical use? For my part I really believe that studies on the physical constitution will have to learn a great deal from astrology; for the body does not shape the soul, but vice-versa.

The idea of the *constellation* of the character has very wide consequences. And now that one of the most competent scholars in physical illnesses—the great Freiburg pathologist Aschoff— has come out and spoken in favor of astrology, perhaps those persons who incline to an interest in the intangible and the psyche will not be so rejecting of astrology or of considering the material I have presented here.

But I can readily add—so that enthusiasm does not get out of hand—that one can more easily become a competent and perhaps even good analyst than become a proficient astrologer. Most of the astrology one encounters every day can in no way be considered worthwhile for serious psychoanalytic or scientific use. Astrologers must first know something about psychoanalysis, which was the reason that I used such a controversial subject as a basis for this work, for material which is useful for psychoanalysis is not generally to be found among the astrological interpretations that are usually encountered.

Can one expect much of psychoanalysis and astrology joined together? It is very much a matter of being able to see the essentials for the past and the present at the same time. This is the demand of analysis as well as its goal. These are the high requirements to which it must be educated. But to know the future—or to be able to know it? Perhaps the lines ". . . und begehre nimmer und nimmer zu schauen, was die Gotter gnadig bedecken mit Nacht und Grauen" are more valid for the future than the forgotten or repressed elements of the past. But in any case, an important conclusion is that the amateurs can cause more harm than good in astrology just as in psychoanalysis, and much of astrological knowledge is suitable only for the doctor.

Without intuition there will be no adept at psychoanalysis but only mediocrity; without a knowledge of combination and synthesis there will be no adept at astrology.